visible mending

**Repair, Renew, Reuse
The Clothes You Love**

Photography by Arounna Khounnoraj

AROUNNA KHOUNNORAJ

Hardie Grant

QUADRILLE

introduction

What does it mean to mend? For most people it means to repair, patch or rebuild – it's about making something whole again. And it's also about the activity and utility of mending, through intention and necessity, to make something useful again. One thing is for sure, though: it is not about replacing something old with something new.

Mending textiles and clothing has always been an important part of past practises. We mended because we had to; it was a natural part of the useful life of things. As fabric became worn, mending was the next step in extending its life: creation, use, mending and reuse. Every culture that has a history of textiles also has a history of mending, and each with its own approach. Often reflective of social context, techniques evolved to make the need for mending as acceptable as possible – from the overtly decorative to the virtually invisible. From the traditions of boro, sashiko or kantha to different types of darning, weaving and patching, mending fulfilled our needs but also offered a sense of beauty and of understanding for textiles and clothes and how we use them. Mending is a part of all places and all families.

In more recent years our relationship with mending has changed and for many consumers it plays a much smaller role in our lives – and in quite a few cases no role at all. Affluence and the textile industry as a whole have made it unnecessary and, in fact, have fostered a relationship with fabric where replacing worn items became the norm. And yet, for contemporary makers, mending techniques continue to have a place in our studio practises.

I have always loved patchwork, assemblage and collage. They can be evocative of so many things – the quality of torn edges, the honesty of fabrication or the beauty of worn or incomplete things. Whether repairing something old, or using old fabric to create something new, mending returns a value to something. It's an opportunity to decorate, express identity and celebrate connections. It's an extension of making, but also an opportunity for expression.

how to use this book

I've divided this book into two main areas: a tools and techniques section, followed by the projects. The mending techniques and stitches that I use are hand-sewing techniques, which you can apply in a variety of situations – and each is given their own individual focus in the techniques section, so you can learn the basics and a little history.

Although the techniques form the foundations with which we will work, I should talk a bit about how they relate to the projects that I've chosen. Because mending is such a broad subject, I wanted the projects to reflect this by offering a range of creative possibilities that use the techniques in different ways and for different purposes. So I've also organized the projects into three categories: repair, renew and reuse.

Repair is the closest to traditional mending, using a variety of techniques such as sashiko, patching or darning. These projects are exactly as they sound – repairing old and worn items in creative ways that extend their lives and allow the mending to express something about each item.

Renew is when you have a piece of clothing that is otherwise fine, but just seems tired and needs a little something. Here we will use some of our favourite techniques, such as stitching, dyeing, surface design or appliqué, to decorate and revive these pieces and bring them back to life.

Reuse is how I describe the making of something altogether new using old fabric and remnants, old items reinterpreted in new ways, or using traditional mending techniques in new situations.

In all the projects I describe the techniques and materials that I've chosen and give you step-by-step instructions to show how I worked. While working you can also refer back to the techniques section for specific details about individual techniques or stitches.

For some projects you will be able to make something quite like my example; in others my examples are in many ways merely suggestions, which you can apply or adapt to suit one of your garments. Feel free to take your own course, choosing the techniques or stitches that you feel work. Remember: mending is about bringing your items back to life, reinterpreting them and – above all – not wasting, so using what you have on hand is key. So don't worry if your material or colour choices differ from mine. In the end I hope that each project or technique will give you a skill set, and inspiration to carry on with your own projects and designs.

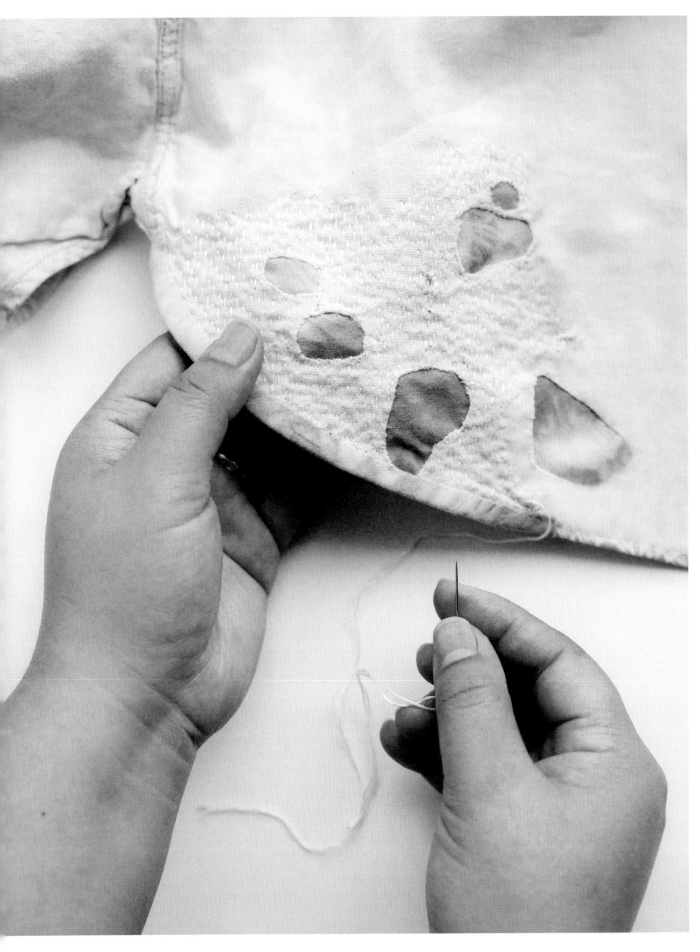

why mend?

I can think of lots of reasons why I mend, but there are a couple that stand out. To start with, mending and mending techniques are activities that I've always done. They're at the heart of any creative studio, making things by hand with fabric and thread, finding a vision. Even before I had a studio, when I was a child, my mother made our clothes out of necessity. Not all of them, but a lot. So working with bits of borrowed fabric was a part of my earliest experiences, and working with material, paper and thread followed me through several art schools and remains with me today. Whether I'm reworking old clothes or incorporating old techniques to make my products, mending has an ethos that I'm sure all makers understand. It's a part of working and thinking with your hands – cutting and sewing layers and layers, and stitch by stitch holding it all together.

Of all the things I do in the studio, patchwork is one of my favourites. I love the process and I love the aesthetic of combining patterns and drawings into some sort of whole – it's endlessly creative. It's also something that comes easily to me, because I have lots of fabric around. Why? Because I never waste fabric that can be used for something, so I try always to save my scraps and remnants.

I've always believed in an 'economy of means' in art practice, where everything is just what it needs to be, nothing more, nothing less, and nothing wasted. And avoiding waste is a concept that is central to mending.

Which leads us to another thought. The truth is that most people have very little creative connection to the clothing they wear. The textile industry taught us not to. We've grown accustomed to the endless cycle of consumption, with seasonal offerings made in other places with faceless labour. We regard items as virtually disposable pieces to be used or worn and then discarded. The out-of-pocket prices are low, but there is always a larger price to be paid.

The textile and clothing industry as a whole plays a significant part in the global economy. As concerns over climate change are inescapable, it's time to realize that over-consumption, over-production and waste in the textile industry are major contributors to the carbon emissions connected to climate change. Agriculture, manufacturing, chemical production, transportation around the world – there are energy needs with every step, leading to an enormous environmental impact. The bottom line is that 'fast fashion' has left us with a very different world. While we long for endless creativity, we're left with endless disposability – with almost nothing recyclable.

Obviously this is not news: we all need to adopt sustainable patterns of consumption in all parts of our lives, and our relationship to clothing is no exception. As individuals some things are difficult to change – but changing how we consume may be within our grasp. Experts in climate change and global economics have suggested that by making personal consumer choices we can make a meaningful impact on our environment. In the report *The Future of Urban Consumption in a 1.5°C World* by C40 Cities, Arup and the University of Leeds, it was suggested that reducing our clothing purchases to eight new items a year would cut supply chain waste by 50% and achieve climate change goals in the textile industry by the year 2050. And if you're up for a real challenge and you reduce your purchases to three new items per year, that would cut supply chain waste by 75%.

But there are options and there are plenty of caring and creative people out there doing amazing things. So maybe it's time to embrace a new, or renewed, connection with the textiles

and clothing items in our lives. Taking care, mending and being creative with what we already have might be one way to ensure our journey continues in the right direction.

essential equipment

You don't need a lot of equipment for needlework; you can start with this simple list. And while it's fair to say that quality tools and materials can make a difference, in the spirit of mending I'd say that if you have something else that will do at a pinch then by all means use it. One thing I would recommend is a quality needle; despite its size, a needle is probably the most important item on the list. It will always be in your hand and good needles really do perform better, which will make things easier and more enjoyable.

NEEDLES

For hand sewing and mending, needles are going to be your most used tool. You will need a mixture of sewing and darning needles, preferably quality ones that glide through fabric. They come in various sizes but I use needles that are at least 4cm (1½in) long because they are more comfortable to hold. I store my needles in a needle book or a tubular case so as to keep their tips from getting damaged.

Sharps

Sharps are all-purpose hand-sewing needles; they're good for appliqué, patching and mending. They tend to be sharper and thinner in order to go through layers of cloth easily.

Embroidery

Embroidery needles have a bigger eye that you can put thicker threads through.

Sashiko

Sashiko needles are longer with a bigger eye for thicker threads. The longer length of the needle allows you to load on several stitches at once, making the stitching quicker.

Tapestry

These needles come in metal and plastic and are typically blunt with a large eye; they are commonly used for cross stitch and tapestry. They're ideal for darning knitwear because the blunt tip slides through the knitted fabric easily without splitting the yarn, and the big eye can accommodate thicker yarns better.

THREADS/YARN

When it comes to threads or yarn there are some typical rules regarding how and where to use certain types, but to be honest these rules can easily be broken. Usually I try to match the yarn or thread to the garment that I am working on, so if it's a knitted wool garment I tend to use a wool yarn of similar weight. I like to use tapestry wool when I need a heavier thread to repair socks or sweaters – it's available in small skeins and in so many colours. To repair woven fabrics or denim I use cotton embroidery thread (floss), which is composed of a number of strands (typically six) so it has a nice weight and you can separate out fewer strands if you want a finer line of stitching. For topstitching (see page 18) on projects I like to use sashiko threads because they are spun together tightly so they create a firm line; they also tend to be a bit duller and less shiny, which I prefer for some garments.

However, I also think you should use what you have, and if you really want your mending to stand out it might make sense to use a contrasting thread or yarn. The great thing about darning is that there is such a variety of materials that you could use, so often it comes down to a matter of taste and experimentation. Mixing and matching is always fun, and because you don't always need a lot of yarn or thread for repairs or detailwork you have a perfect reason to keep all your leftovers. I keep a stash of yarn from past projects and I look to that first before considering buying more.

DARNING MUSHROOM

This is a wooden object the shape of a mushroom to assist you when you are hand mending, because it can be awkward to hold a garment while darning. It's held under the area to be mended with one hand to provide a surface for the needle to work against. You can find darning mushrooms in vintage shops and knitting stores, and they come in different shapes and sizes depending on the location of the mend you need to repair. Small ones for the tight areas of socks and gloves are called darning eggs. If you don't have one, as an alternative you can use a glass jar or a tennis ball. I find it's also helpful to use an elastic band to hold the garment down on to the darning mushroom.

EMBROIDERY HOOP

Embroidery hoops are frames to stretch the fabric while you are darning, doing appliqué, or working embroidery. Hoops have two parts: an inner circle placed under the fabric and an outer circle placed on top and tightened with a screw to hold the fabric taut. These are the best tools to isolate an area to work on, keeping it tight and pucker free, but they work best on woven fabrics that don't have a lot of stretch.

WATER-SOLUBLE FABRIC PENCIL

Also known as a washable tailor's pencil. There will be many times when you will need to draw directly onto the projects you are working on in order to organize your stitch lines – such as for sashiko, laying down a design to follow with embroidery, or to make sewing marks on dark fabric. Washable pencils come in different colours and, when you are finished, just give your fabric a rinse and the pencil marks will disappear.

PINS/SAFETY PINS

You'll need plenty of pins to hold layers of cloth together when working on your designs, as well as when sewing. Safety pins are good for larger areas or for items that will be sitting on your lap, while straight pins are better for when you are machine sewing or when you need to quickly hold down a piece of fabric. As an alternative, when you have pretty much decided what goes where, you can also use a needle and thread and tack (baste) down the layers (see page 18).

FABRIC SCISSORS AND THREAD SNIPS

A pair of good scissors is crucial for all forms of fabric cutting. Thread snips are small scissors with no handle that are good for cutting small areas or for cutting threads. Only use your scissors on fabric or threads and keep a separate pair for cutting paper.

SEAM RIPPER

This tool has a small tip and a hook-shaped blade and has plenty of uses. It quickly cuts through stitching along a seam while you are deconstructing a garment, or when you've changed your mind and want to try something else in your stitching. It is also perfect for getting into areas that are too small for scissors.

WOOD SEAM ROLLER

I used to use an iron to flatten my seams while sewing or patching, but that meant going back and forth to the iron and heating it up. Recently I started using a seam roller instead, a cylinder made of wood or plastic with a handle that is used to roll your seams flat after you have opened them up; having flat seam helps to keep your work neat. Seam rollers come in different widths but I find the 2.5cm (1in) or 4cm (1½in) ones are good sizes to use.

THIMBLE

There are many kinds of thimble, all of which help you to move a needle through fabric by making a little cap for one of your fingers. Metal thimbles are typically used for pushing the needle, but I sometimes use rubber thimbles on my forefinger and thumb, which also helps me to grip the needle while I pull it through the fabric. A sashiko thimble is worn a bit lower on the finger so that you aren't using your fingertip when pushing the needle. This can be helpful when you have a lot of stitching, which can sometimes be tiring.

BEESWAX

Depending on your fabric, some threads can be difficult to pull though – especially when there are several layers. Running your thread through beeswax can help the thread glide through the cloth easily.

NEEDLE FELTING TOOLS

Needles used for felting wool roving have little burrs along the sides of the lower portion, which help grab and push the wool roving into the fabric. They also have a wider upper portion with a little bend at the top to make it easy to hold them between two fingers. Some makers bundle together several needles to speed up the process, although I prefer to use a single needle. You will also need a soft surface to work on underneath the item, such as a dense sponge or piece of foam.

STICK 'N' STITCH PAPER/MAGIC PAPER

Some fabrics used for needlework such as embroidery are difficult to draw a pattern on, especially when the pattern is highly detailed. One solution is to print, photocopy or draw your design onto this water-soluble paper, which adheres to the surface of your fabric. With your design image visible you stitch right through it to the fabric below. Once finished, you simply run it under the tap (faucet) and water washes the paper away, leaving your work behind.

GLUE

White glue or glue sticks can come in handy for many reasons, such as for applying to a cut edge to stop the fabric from fraying or to tack down pieces while you are stitching.

sewing stitches

Stitches are one of the most important parts of our work – they hold everything together, and so many different mending techniques rely on the same simple stitches common to all hand sewing. However, there are different ways to think about stitches. On a fundamental level, most stitches are used for specific reasons – such as for edging, or to join together layers of fabric in different ways. But when used for mending, stitches go beyond their use purely as a means to construct. Even standard stitches have a graphic quality that elevates them to important design elements; they are not just a means to an end but a means for expression as well. Stitchwork is equal to the lines of a drawing – the type and colour of threads used, the scale and spacing of the stitch, whether straight, irregular or combined in different ways: all these will have an effect on the final result.

RUNNING STITCH

This is probably the most basic stitch that you will use in hand sewing – and for mending it's probably the one you will use the most. In appearance it resembles a continuous line composed of little dashes.

1 First thread your needle and tie a knot at the end, then pull the thread through the fabric from underneath until the knot hits the fabric.

2 Start by 'loading' stitches onto your needle – about three at a time, depending on the length of the needle – in an under and over movement, and then pull the thread through to get the resulting dashes. Repeat as many times as necessary.

3 By loading the needle you will work faster than working one stitch at a time. I usually try to keep the distance between stitches equal to the length of the stitches, but you can modify the spacing for visual impact.

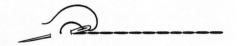

TOPSTITCHING

This is a form of running stitch that is worked from the good side very close to an edge as a decorative feature, and also to keep the layers correctly aligned at the edge. I like to use sashiko threads for topstitching, as they give a crisp line.

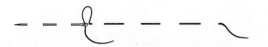

TACKING/BASTING

Tacking (basting) is a loose form of a running stitch, with the visible thread of the stitch much longer (about 2.5cm/1in long). It's a temporary stitch worked using standard thread to hold layers together until the permanent stitching is worked; it's usually removed when you have finished your piece. I tend to use a thread colour that stands out so it doesn't get confused with the design that I'm working on.

BACKSTITCH

This stitch appears as a continuous line because the individual stitches have small or no spaces between them. It's especially useful when making imagery, as in embroidery, or when you want your stitches to have the graphic quality of a line. It's called backstitch because the needle alternates between a forward and a backward direction.

1 First thread your needle and tie a knot at the end, then pull the thread through the fabric from underneath until the knot hits the fabric. Make one stitch in a forward direction.

2 With the needle now underneath, bring it back through to the top one stitch length ahead of the end of the previous stitch. Next, rather than continuing forward, insert the needle back into the end of the previous stitch, making the stitch line appear unbroken.

3 With the needle underneath again, bring it back through to the top two stitch lengths forward, and then back again by one stitch length into the end of the last stitch. Continuing with two spaces forward underneath, one space back on top, results in a continuous line of stitches.

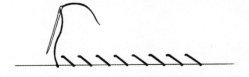 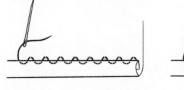

WHIP STITCH

Whip stitch is similar to running stitch in that it is a continuous line of stitches with visible spaces between. But rather than appearing as a series of dashes in a single direction, the stitches are worked either on an angle or perpendicular to the stitch line. While whip stitch could be used anywhere, it is more commonly used along fabric edges – such as to join two or more layers of fabric together, or to attach smaller pieces of fabric onto larger pieces.

1 The edge of the fabric could be rolled under to form a neat finish or left raw. Start your whip stitch underneath in the usual way and then bring the needle up through both layers you wish to join, near to the edge you will be working over.

2 Make a stitch over the edge in a diagonal direction or perpendicular to the edge, then take the needle sideways underneath and up through the fabric to make the next stitch. Repeat until the edges of the fabric are sewn together.

SLIP/BLIND STITCH

A slip or blind stitch is different from many other stitches outlined here in that its purpose is to be as invisible as possible. This is a good stitch for closing openings where you have turned an item right side out after sewing, or when you are sewing the binding onto an edge. In all cases at least one neatly folded edge is necessary to work through, so that the stitches can be hidden within the fold.

1 First thread your needle and tie a knot at the end, then pull the thread through the point of the folded edge from inside the fold until the knot hits the fabric.

2 Take a tiny stitch into the base fabric you are sewing onto, or into the opposite fold if you are sewing two edges together. If you are sewing into a base fabric, use only the tip of your needle to take the stitch so it is as small as possible.

3 Take the next stitch into the folded edge and out again a bit further along. Repeat this back and forth, moving along within the fold – or both folds – each time, to create a ladder-like stitch, which when gently tugged will pull the two sides together.

 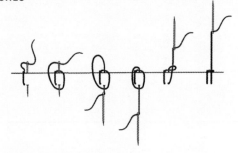

BLANKET STITCH

This is a very versatile and expressive stitch that can be used along the edges of fabric to create a finished edge that is decorative from both sides. Blanket stitches can also be used to emphasize the edges of openings and for neatening the edges of random little holes from wear and tear. In most cases blanket stitches maintain consistent spacing and entry/exit points for the needle, but feel free to experiment.

1 The first stitch won't be a true blanket stitch but a way of anchoring your thread. Begin by tying a knot at the end of the thread and then push the needle from the back of your fabric to the front about 5mm (¼in) from the edge (the spacing is really up to you though). Wrap the needle and thread around the edge and come up through the same hole again so that you have now created a loop around the edge. To finish the anchor, slide your needle sideways along the edge of the fabric and underneath the stitch you just made.

2 Now start the true blanket stitch by pushing the needle into the fabric from back to front, again 5mm (¼in) from the edge and 5mm (¼in) further along from your anchor stitch. Pull the thread almost through, leaving a loop, then take the needle down through the loop and gently pull to complete the stitch. Repeat the blanket stitches until you have finished the entire perimeter of your piece.

BUTTONHOLE STITCH/
TAILOR'S BUTTONHOLE STITCH

Buttonhole stitch has similar characteristics to blanket stitch but the spacing is much closer and at the top edge there is an extra purl, a little knot that secures the stitches in place and keeps the fabric from fraying through use. Also in buttonhole stitch the needle will be pointing toward you – this is key, because it allows you to wrap the thread around both ends of the needle before it is pulled out fully.

1 Knot your thread and establish a stitch line parallel to the buttonhole opening. Typically buttonhole stitches are small, perhaps 3mm (⅛in), but it's really up to you. Push the needle through the buttonhole opening and up from the back of the fabric at a point along the stitch line; pull it all the way out until the knot hits the fabric.

2 To begin buttonhole stitch, insert the needle into the buttonhole and out through the stitch line just to the left and very close to where you started. Before you pull your needle all the way through, wrap the thread behind the top of the needle going right and then run it underneath the tip of the needle going left, and then run it underneath the tip of the needle going right, so that you are creating a loop around the needle from the previous stitch.

3 Holding the thread just to the right of the needle tip with your thumb to keep it from getting tangled, pull the needle through – but before you tighten it all the way, pull the needle and thread upward and away from you so that the resulting knot sits at the top along the edge of the buttonhole.

4 Repeat along the buttonhole; as the stitches grow, the little knots will form a line along the edge. Fan the stitches at one end to create the curve the button will sit in.

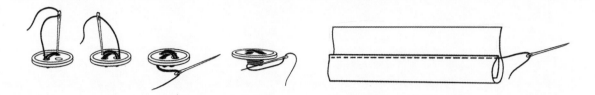

SEWING ON A BUTTON

The technique for this is basically the same for a two-hole or a four-hole button. With a four-hole button you can make your stitches in an 'X' as described below, or in two parallel lines. If your button has a plain flat top and a loop underneath, you just sew it on through the loop.

1 Begin with a very large knot on your thread and pull the needle and thread through from the back of the cloth at the point that you want the button located. Take the needle through one of the holes in the button until the button is sitting on the fabric.

2 Next, bring the needle down through the opposite hole and into the fabric, then up again through the same hole you started with. Repeat this, coming up and down about four times, keeping the threads a little loose as you go.

3 If your button only has two holes, take the thread down through one of the holes but not through the fabric, and wind it around the stitches tightly four times to create a shank below the button to accommodate the thickness of the buttonhole. Then take the thread through the fabric and secure on the back with a knot as described below.

4 If your button has four holes, then move to the empty holes and sew another four times until your stitches result in an 'X'. Create the shank as described in step 3. Now take the needle through the fabric to the back and pull the needle under and over into the fabric until you form a loop. Pull the needle through the loop and pull to make a knot. Repeat a second time and then snip the thread.

DOUBLE HEM

To create a hem, fold over the edge by 5mm (¼in) and then by another 5mm (¼in) so that the raw edge of the fabric is tucked inside. Sew in place close to the inner folded edge with running stitch or use slip/blind stitch for a more invisible hem.

ESSENTIAL MENDING TECHNIQUES

essential mending techniques

As many ways as there are of making cloth, fabric and textiles, there are as many ways to mend. And if we add in all the different stitches and sewing techniques, then we have quite a long list – an entire history of needlework, in fact. History might also suggest that certain techniques and stitches are most suitable for certain types of fabric only, but you'd have to be a historian to sort it out and in my work I don't always follow the rules. For most of us there are a few fundamental approaches that are suitable for many different situations. In this section you will find all the basic techniques to give you a full range of possibilities, but I've also focused on techniques that are mostly visible. These will give you a multitude of ways to celebrate the mend by emphasizing colour contrast, weight of material or fabric pattern. Once you become comfortable with these techniques, feel free to experiment and use each one to your liking.

darning

Darning is one of the most common forms of mending, and it was standard practice at one time to darn holes to prolong the life of fabric items. For me, woven darning is probably one of my favourite techniques to use because in many ways it is such a pure expression of mending – especially for someone who loves needlework. With this technique, a single thread or yarn is interwoven into the existing grain and becomes one with the existing fabric. Duplicate stitch darning is mainly used on knitted fabrics – with this you recreate or duplicate the knitted stitches, thus strengthening the existing fabric. And finally, blanket stitch can also easily be used as a darning stitch to fill in holes in woven or knitted fabric, creating an effect that resembles crochet. All these forms have the ability to visibly stand out to create a new dialogue with an old garment.

DARNING WEAVING

Woven darning can be simple to fine, visible to invisible, but most types use what is commonly referred to as a darning stitch, which adds a mini woven section over the damaged area. The darning stitch creates a warp and weft with thread or yarn, which are anchored into the existing fabric on all sides of the mend. It is most suitable where the damage is a hole or weakness due to wear, and because darning weaving extends into the weave of a fabric it is typically used for knitwear, woven fabrics and denim. At its most basic, there are a couple of ways that I use this technique. Both mend a hole in the fabric; the difference is in how the stitches are anchored. In the first method, sometimes referred to as darning weave with seeds, the anchor stitches extend some way into the existing fabric creating little dashes or seed stitches surrounding the hole. This reinforces a larger area around the hole, making it more durable – but it also has an aesthetic effect because the dense weave over the actual hole contrasts with the radiant field of stitches. The second approach, simply referred to as a darning weave, takes the stitches into the existing fabric only as far as necessary to create a connection. In this case the woven mend appears as a more distinct and specific shape filling in the gap – often a square, as a result of the weave.

Darning weave with seed stitches

1 In order to create a work surface, place a darning mushroom or a similarly curved object underneath the garment and centred to the hole. Use an elastic band to hold the garment in place (refer to the step images on pages 28–29). Choose a starting point some distance below and to one side of the hole. Thread your tapestry needle with wool yarn and push the needle up from the back to the front, leaving a 7.5cm (3in) or so tail that you will later weave into the back when you have finished the entire mend. Leave a similar tail at the back whenever you need to start a new thread as well.

2 For the warp, start working a line of small running stitches parallel to the weave of the existing fabric and continue it up, making little dashes of yarn, to a point above and beyond the hole – the distance is up to you, but it is usually symmetrical to the distance you started below the hole. Now reverse direction and continue your line of stitches back down, close to the previous line. Continue working up and down, trying to begin and end the lines of seed stitches somewhat randomly.

3 When you have worked to the hole, on the next line of stitches you need to create one long stitch that will reach across the hole and into the fabric on the other side. Continue in this way upward and downward across the width of the hole, remembering to keep your stitches over the hole close together as this is where the weaving will be so you want the area to be dense. Continue creating the seed stitches above and below the hole as before.

4 On the other side of the hole, continue working a line of small running stitches into the existing fabric, as you did at the start, until you feel you are far enough away from the hole.

5 You will now repeat this entire process to create the weft, perpendicular to the warp. Again, start in the existing fabric using your running stitch to create lines of little seed stitches. When you get to the hole take your needle over and under the warp threads to create the weave before continuing the seed stitches into the fabric on the opposite side.

6 On the next pass, when you reach the warp threads go under and over – so working alternately to the first pass. Continue this process back and forth, over and under, then under and over, until the hole is completely woven over. Carry on to extend your stitches into the existing fabric as far as you wish. Be careful not to make the tension too tight or the fabric will pucker.

7 When you are finished on the front, turn the piece over to clean up any loose ends of yarn. To avoid making knots, thread any loose yarn tails into your needle, one by one, and weave them into the backs of your running stitches. This will keep your stitches from coming undone and be more comfortable when wearing the garment.

Darning weave without seed stitches

1 This is in most respects identical to the procedure outlined opposite, except that your stitches only extend into the existing fabric a short distance. First clean the hole by snipping off any loose ends to give the edges a more regular shape. Choose your starting point only a short distance below and to the side of the hole and bring your thread through as in step 1, opposite.

2 Start working running stitches as described in steps 2 to 4, but instead of taking the stitches too far into the surrounding fabric keep the starting and stopping points of each line of stitches a common distance from the hole. This creates a more defined and regular edge to the mend, with the woven area sometimes geometric, but possibly organic, depending on how you want it to appear.

3 When you have finished the warp, create the weft as in steps 5 and 6 – again starting and stopping near the hole until a dense woven shape covering the hole is complete. Finish the back by working any loose ends into the weave as in step 7 opposite.

DARNING WEAVE WITH SEED STITCHES

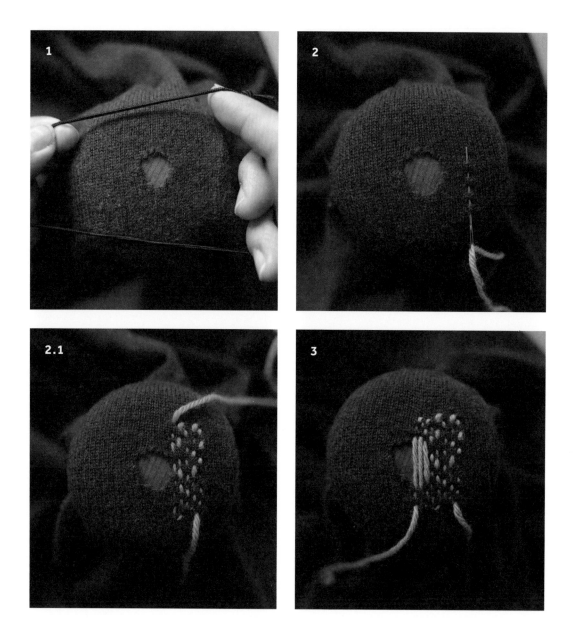

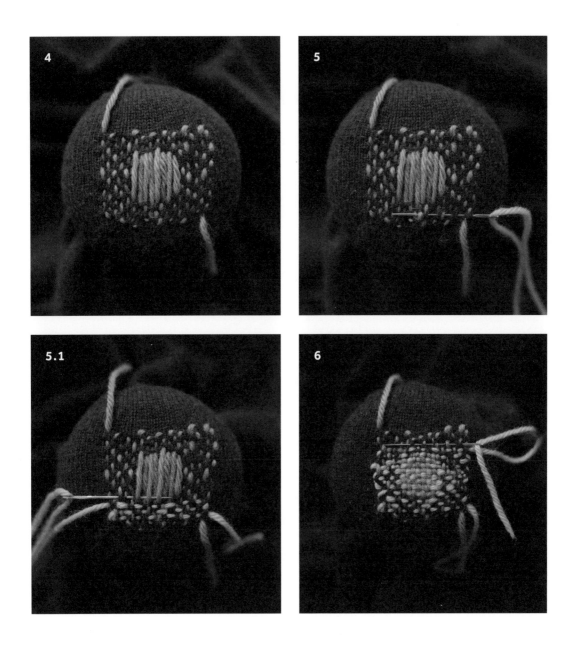

DUPLICATE STITCH

This type of darning is generally used to mend stocking (stockinette) stitch knitted garments using a tapestry needle and yarn. It works best on areas of knitwear that have thinned out due to wear, but have not yet developed actual holes. It's a preventative measure that reinforces the structure of the knit – and because of that it is usually best to choose a similar yarn to that used for the garment but, if possible, slightly lighter in weight so it doesn't add too much bulk. Thankfully it's not as daunting as some stitches are, since your guide to follow is right in front of you in the existing knit; you just need to follow along.

1 Thread your tapestry needle with yarn and find a starting point just outside of the worn area – I tend to begin working right to left and upward, so I'll be starting at the bottom right corner. Bring the needle from the back to the front through the middle of an existing knitted stitch so that it appears at the bottom of a 'V'. Leave a tail 5–7cm (2–3in) long on the inside, which you will weave into the back of your work afterwards.

2 Next, follow the existing loop of the knitted stitch up and insert the needle from right to left underneath the two threads of the stitch in the row above. Pull the yarn through, and insert it back into the spot where you started. You have just completed a stitch, or loop that mimics an existing knitted stitch.

3 Now you simply need to repeat the process. So, from the back, move the needle to the next knitted stitch to the left and pull the needle up at the bottom of the next 'V', then as before, follow the loop up, inserting your needle under the two threads of the stitch above and back to the bottom of the 'V' again. Move to the next stitch to the left and repeat until you have completed a row as far as you need to.

4 When it's time to move up to the next row above, instead of moving to the next stitch along, simply bring the needle from the back to the front up through the middle of the stitch above. Continue working, now moving from left to right.

5 Repeat these steps until the area is filled. Because you're duplicating the knit rather than replacing it with something altogether different, it's possible to make a mend that is potentially invisible if you choose the same yarn as used for the existing item. But keep in mind that your mend can also stand out through using a different colour and by how you organize your rows to create shapes or patterns.

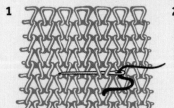
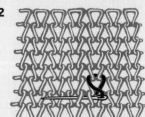
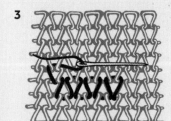
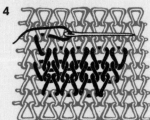

BLANKET STITCH

More often blanket stitches are used as a decorative finish along the outer edges of fabric, quite often one with unfinished edges. But it can also easily be used as a darning stitch to fill in holes.

1 Start by cleaning any loose ends around the edge of the hole. Thread your tapestry needle with any tapestry wool or yarn similar to the garment. Starting anywhere along the hole and a short distance from the edge, push the tapestry needle through from the back to the front, leaving a 7.5cm (3in) tail on the inside that will later be woven into the mend.

2 As with a basic blanket stitch (see page 20), create a starting loop by wrapping the yarn around the edge and coming up through the same hole again so that you have now created a loop around the edge. Slide your needle sideways along the edge of the fabric and underneath the stitch you just made to anchor the thread.

3 Now bring the needle from back to front next to the last stitch. Bring the needle up to the edge and through the loop from the previous stitch. Pull tight. You have completed the first blanket stitch, so repeat it all around the edge of the hole until you return to your starting point.

4 For the next row you will be repeating the blanket stitch but rather than anchoring the stitches into the existing fabric you will work them into the previous row of stitches. Continue in this way around and around, row by row. Keep in mind that, because you will be working in a circular manner, you will need to reduce the number of stitches on each row by stitching onto every other stitch of the previous row in order to keep the stitches flat as you work towards the centre. Continue in this manner until the hole is filled in. When filled, turn your piece over and thread any loose tails into the mend as explained in step 7 on page 26.

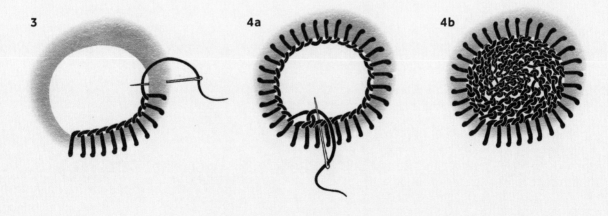

3   4a   4b

binding

Some projects in this book have binding only along a short section, others have binding all around the edge in a continuous strip. If you are binding all around an item such as a quilt, you will need to deal with the corners and with finishing the ends.

Binding an edge

1 Cut a strip of fabric about 5cm (2in) wide. If you are going to bind a longer edge, cut more strips and join them together to make a longer length of binding.

2 Line up one raw edge of the binding with the raw edge of the item, with right sides together, and pin in place about every 15cm (6in). Before beginning to sew, fold over the starting end of the binding by about 1cm (⅜in) – this will prevent a frayed edge.

3 Sew the binding in place with a 12mm (½in) seam allowance. At the other end, fold over the end by about 1cm (⅜in) again.

4 Now take the binding strip and wrap it around the edge, folding under the raw edge and pinning it down about every 15cm (6in). Blind stitch (see page 19) the folded edge of the binding down.

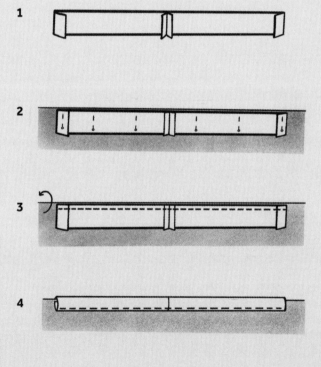

Binding all around

1 Make your binding as in step 1, opposite, joining pieces to make a strip long enough to go all around the item with extra to spare. Begin binding in the middle of one side, as in step 2.

2 At a corner you can either do a mitre corner or a straight corner. To create a mitre corner, stop sewing 12mm (½in) before the corner and fold the binding strip away at a 90-degree angle to the item so that its edge is parallel with the next edge to be bound and you've created a 45-degree angle at the corner.

3 Then fold the strip back to line up with the next raw edge, so that it lies over the triangle fold. Continue sewing around, repeating the mitre on all the corners.

4 Once you have sewn the binding on the front around the perimeter of the quilt, overlap the end over the folded end at the start. Then, fold the binding strip to wrap it around the edge all round. Now, working from the back, fold the binding strip edge once over about 12mm (½in) so that the frayed edges are tucked under and pin in place. To create the corners on the back, press the corner flat to create a 45-degree angle, fold the raw edge under, and then fold the sides down to create a clean mitred corner.

5 When the entire perimeter is folded under, neatly secure with blind stitch (see page 19) all around.

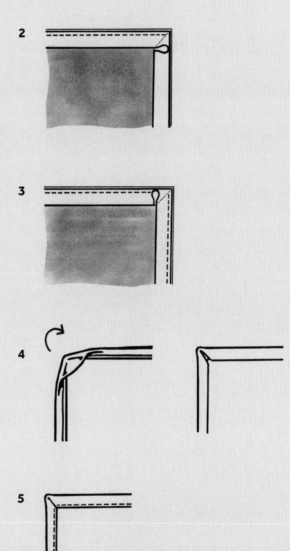

patching

Patching is one of the most basic ways of mending. Simply put, it's repairing a hole or worn area by covering it over with some sort of fabric, stitching around the edge to attach it to the fabric below. But the simplicity of the patch can be misleading because it offers a way to compose surface designs using fabric and stitches and, as such, it's full of artistic possibilities. Patching is about collage and juxtaposition, creating a surface that introduces colours, patterns and tones. It's about both mending and decorating a surface, either by continuing the original idea or introducing a completely different theme. It's about play and contrast. In other words it can be anything you want. As a starting point, there are two basic ways to patch: placing the patch over the hole or weakened area, or placing it underneath the hole. Each method will change the look of the piece in very different ways and offer different possibilities to the maker.

PATCHING ON TOP
When the patch is on top you have more freedom to play with shape, and it can also be layered with other pieces of cloth to create a colourful or patterned surface.

1 Cut a piece of fabric to cover the hole. It can be any shape you like, as long as it is larger all around than the hole itself. Place the patch over the hole and pin in place.

2 There are a couple of obvious ways to treat the edges of any fabric patch. First is to leave the raw edges of the cloth exposed, which means that any stitching that you do will seem almost independent. With this method, just sew around the patch with whip stitch (see page 19), or work lines of sashiko stitching (see page 43) all across it to hold it in place.

3 Alternatively you can tuck the edges under to achieve a cleaner, more finished edge. In this case you can use any of several types of stitch around the edge, such as a simple running stitch, blanket stitch, slip/blind stitch or whip stitch (see pages 16–20).

4 Coloured threads can also be used for stitching that stands out – for these types of patching I would use sashiko or embroidery thread (floss). I find hand stitching gives the mend a handmade look that seems more organic and that celebrates the evidence of the hand.

PATCHING ON TOP

1

2

3

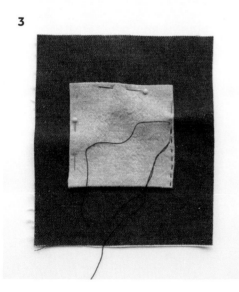

4

PATCHING BENEATH

Of course colour and pattern can equally express themselves from below, but when you place the patch below the hole remains as a visible part of the mend – which automatically emphasizes the hole's qualities as part of the aesthetic experience. The shape, its texture and materiality remain as part of the visible surface and speak of the more ephemeral qualities of fabric like time, history, work and change.

1 Before starting, determine how you want the hole to appear. It can be left raw or can be finished by tucking the edges under to give a clean shape. Cut the patch larger all around than the hole. Centre it below the hole and pin in place.

2 If you plan to leave the edge raw, secure the patch in place by working a simple running stitch (see page 16) around the hole, or work sashiko stitching (see page 43) over the whole area as in step 2 on page 34.

3 For a finished edge, tuck the edge of the hole under with the tip of your needle as you work around the hole. You can work whip stitch or blind stitch (see page 19) to hold the folded edge down.

4 Finally, whip stitch the outer edges as shown on page 39 to hold the patch in place an create a decorative border.

PATCHWORK

When a patch is combined with other patches it leads to patchwork, a technique that I use all the time. For me patchwork goes beyond the singular mend and is about using all my remnants and smaller pieces, sewing them together to build a larger area of fabric. The patchwork fabric can then be used to make various items like scarves, blankets, pillows or bags. An example of a cultural influence for patchwork is boro, a Japanese technique of mending garments by adding small pieces of fabric, which accumulate over time from generation to generation until the item is highly patched. The name derives from the Japanese term for ragged or tattered, and suggests surfaces made of patches of various sizes or patterns, simply stitched in place regardless of any compositional concerns. Originally boro was practised out of economic necessity by the peasant classes using remnants or spare fragments of cloth. As a result, this form of patchwork signified lower or working class origins. Today, however, patchwork carries an aesthetic and meaning that is quite different and even desirable. Not only are these fabrics incredibly beautiful in a visual way, but their appearance, techniques and references remind us of all the meaningful qualities inherent to hand made.

Of course patchwork is evident in every culture and there are many variations evident in the long history of quilting – where it's not so much about layering or accumulation as it is about the aesthetics of composition, form and structure. Here you will find organized patterns and repetitions, quite often with their own names, where each piece of fabric plays a part in the creation of a larger composition that is calculated and designed.

Or there are more organic compositions that grow as they are made; where the maker decides as they work, where there are rules but also exceptions.

For me, patchwork results from decision making that is more intuitive; where I have the freedom to make compositions that express pattern and organization but also contrast, variation, and change.

1 First gather your fabrics and consider your composition. There are many ways to organize patchwork, from regular structures to random groupings. Visual interest is achieved through contrast of form; smaller areas can have activity and a focus and larger areas can be simpler where the eye can rest. I like to achieve a balance between an organized structure and a looser organic form by starting with a small shape, usually a square or a rectangle, and adding pieces around it almost like a spiral, adding larger pieces as the spiral grows.

2 In terms of colour, I like to patch pieces with a monochromatic colour scheme. That way I know the colours will all work together and I can focus on the overall structure of the patching. Working this way lets me play with combinations of light and dark, but also gives the opportunity for the occasional colour or printed fabric remnant to really stand out even if it is just a small little piece of fabric.

3 When you are happy with your arrangement, take a photo as a record to work from. Pick up the first two pieces, place them right sides together and sew along one edge with a 1cm (⅜in) seam allowance, using a needle and thread or the sewing machine. Open out and press the seam flat. Continue with the next piece in the same manner. Depending on your composition, you can sew piece by piece until your patchwork grows, or sew several smaller blocks of patchwork first and then join them together afterward.

PATCHING BENEATH

1

1.1

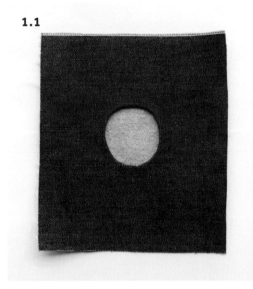

3

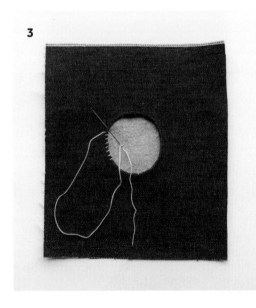

3.1

4

4.1

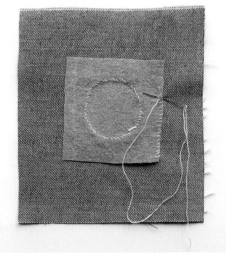

4.2

4.3

appliqué

Appliqué is a technique that is similar in many ways to patching. Both techniques can be used to mend or decorate a surface by using fabric that is shaped and sewn on, and both quite often utilize the same set of stitches. But the intent and effect of appliqué are significantly different; while patching typically uses fabric pieces that are geometric or organic in shape, appliqué is an ornamental form of needlework in which fabric pieces are often used to create a picture, pattern or representational image. Creating a pictorial image or motif, such as flowers or a pattern on top of a garment, allows you to completely renew a piece and create a different kind of visual interest. Appliqué not only achieves the utility of mending, but also lets you redesign older pieces with shape and colour details. There are two approaches to this technique: appliqué and reverse appliqué.

APPLIQUÉ

With this technique, pieces of fabric are applied onto the front surface of the fabric to create a new pattern or design. The shapes of the motifs or patterns can be further emphasized by using contrasting colour or texture fabrics.

1 If you are following a design, you will first need to transfer the different shapes to your appliqué pieces. Tape the template onto a windowpane with the fabric on top. Use a pencil to trace the appliqué shapes onto the fabric. If you want to turn under the edges of your shapes, draw another line 5mm (¼in) outside the first line as your cutting line.

2 Cut out the shapes – following the first line if your shapes will have raw edges, which gives a softer look that emphasizes the nature of the material. Cut along the outer line if you want to turn under the edges of each piece.

3 Arrange the pieces onto the garment in the design. If they will have turned-under edges, pin them in place. If the pieces are to have a raw edge, use pins to hold them in position.

4 A variety of different stitches can be used along the edges of the appliqué pieces, such as blanket stitch, whip stitch or small running stitches (see pages 16–20 for stitches). If the pieces have turned-under edges, it's best to use slip stitch or whip stitch.

5 Additional stitchwork, such as embroidery or sashiko stitching, can be used on top to provide another level of detail to the design.

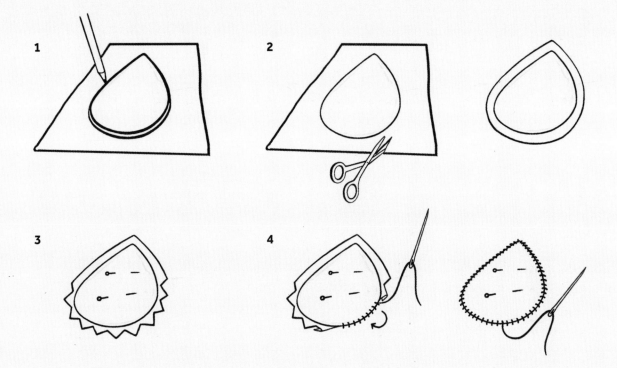

REVERSE APPLIQUÉ

With reverse appliqué the fabric is placed on the back and then made visible by cutting away the surface fabric, which gives it a more recessed look.

1 If you are following a design, you will first need to transfer it to your main fabric. Tape the template onto a windowpane with the fabric on top. Use a pencil to trace the reverse appliqué shapes onto the fabric. If you want to turn under the edges of your shapes, draw another line 5mm (¼in) inside the first line as your cutting line.

2 Cut out the shapes – following the outer line if your shapes will have raw edges, or the inner line if you want to turn under the edges.

3 If you are turning under the edges, first clip around the inside edge of each opening, making sure not to go over the outside line. Make the clips about 5mm (¼in) apart – this clipping will help the edges stay in shape around the curves.

4 Choose the fabric pieces to go behind the holes. If they are close together you can use one piece of cloth to go behind or you can choose different colours or patterns of fabric. Pin the pieces in place behind each opening, or use small scraps of fusible interfacing to hold them in place – making sure to keep them away from the edges so you can still turn these under if you want to.

5 Work a whip stitch or small running stitch (see pages 16–20 for stitches) all around the edge of each opening, using three strands of embroidery thread (floss). If you want to turn the edges under, use the tip of your needle to push the fabric edges under as you work and slip stitch them in place.

6 Tie off with a finishing knot (see page 57). Continue until the fabric edges are tucked under around each opening.

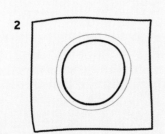
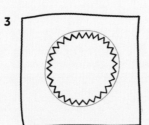

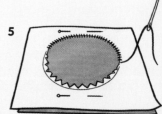

sashiko

Sashiko is a traditional Japanese stitching technique that will be used constantly when you start mending. Meaning 'little stabs' in Japanese, it utilizes small running stitches to create a network of lines on the surface of fabric. Commonly associated with boro (see page 36), this form of embroidery stitching helps to reinforce the surface of the garment as well as to attach patches. When used for boro, sashiko stitches are quite often sewn freehand without the aid of a grid, with the appearance of the stitches reflecting a utilitarian functional need and changing direction as needed. Over time, though, sashiko evolved into a finer form of surface design often with more complex geometric stitching patterns, combining horizontal and vertical stitches. In contemporary use, sashiko can be purely decorative and yet maintains its quality of the handmade. It creates an overall field of stitches across a surface that visually stands out from its surroundings and its linear quality becomes a design element itself.

There are two general categories of sashiko patterns. Moyozashi are interlocking and repeated patterns of shapes created across a surface within an overall grid, which organizes the scale, form and repetition of the shapes. Stitch lines tend to be continuous across the entire surface of a panel, using horizontal, vertical, diagonal and curves, which, as they cross and interlock with each other, highlight the pattern of shapes. Hitomezashi patterns use horizontal or vertical stitch lines only, organized on a grid. The stitches do not create recognizable shapes, but highlight the grid itself by creating a field focusing on the individual stitches such as dashes, crosses, or zigzags – sometimes as interlocking or concentric groupings. Both pattern types use running stitches laid down across the entire surface, carefully laid out using measured and marked lines within the grid. I personally prefer to stitch freehand so I can improvise and adopt a little more freedom in my patterning.

1 There are a number of ways to transfer a starting grid and pattern onto your base fabric. Using a fabric pencil or pen you can draw directly right onto the fabric. A transparent quilter's ruler is best to lay out a regular grid, sized and placed as you wish with your stitches highlighted within the grid.

2 If you have a paper drawing of your pattern, you can scale it to size on a photocopier and transfer it to your fabric by tracing over it with transfer paper underneath. Or you can hold the pattern and your fabric against a light table or a windowpane so you can trace over it. There are also different types of washable or tear-away paper (see page 15) that you can draw or print on and stitch right over, removing the paper once you finish.

3 Sashiko thread is typically used for this type of mending. Unlike other embroidery thread (floss) it is tightly wound for strength and to avoid wear due to fraying. Sashiko needles tend to be sharp and elongated. Traditionally fabrics tend to be natural such as cotton or linen, but to be honest I find any fabric regardless of weight can be used.

4 Thread the needle, and make a tailor's knot at the end (see page 56). Bring the needle through the fabric at your starting point. Since you are primarily using running stitches, you can load the needle with several stitches at a time, saving time and allowing you to be more accurate in spacing.

5 Continue sewing in your desired pattern, keeping the lines evenly spaced if you are working freehand, until you have completed your design. Finish with a finishing knot (see page 57).

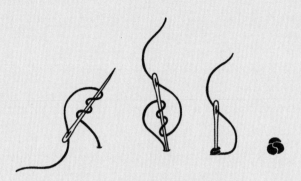

embroidery

In its most general form embroidery is a means to embellish and decorate a fabric's surface with needle and thread, and it is a pretty large category of needlework. I use surface embroidery to add decorative details and elements, shapes and colours, and pictorial elements and patterns in a free-style manner and in conjunction with other techniques such as appliqué. Mending offers many opportunities for using embroidery, such as to embellish and interpret holes in garments by not only reinforcing their edges but also by making them visually stand out with colour and texture. You can also create an embroidered image, either directly on the garment or as a patch – which not only provides a useful mend but also reinterprets the garment in a completely new way, with a collection of handmade images. Embroidery stitches are mainly worked in cotton embroidery thread (floss) or with tapestry wool, but to achieve a level of detail in your work they work better when you are not using very thick threads. Stranded embroidery thread (floss) allows you to use fewer strands for a finer thread. There are hundreds of different embroidery stitches; here are just a few that I use constantly.

French knot

1 Come up through the fabric at the point where you want to place the knot. Wrap the thread around the tip of the needle as many times as you want – more wraps will give a bigger knot.

2 Place the tip of the needle against the fabric right next to where it came out. Push the wraps toward the tip and hold them with a fingertip against the fabric.

3 Keeping the wraps held in place, push the needle through the fabric, causing a decorative knot to form on the surface.

Split stitch

1 A split stitch is ideal for linear elements or for creating outlines around areas and shapes in your embroidery. The split stitch is similar to the backstitch but because the needle comes up within the fibres of the embroidery thread (floss) it results in a fuller, more continuous looking line. Start by making a single stitch.

2 With the needle still underneath, create the next stitch by backing up, bringing the needle up at the mid point of the previous stitch and in between the strands of embroidery thread, thus splitting the thread.

3 Continue by making another stitch forward, and again, coming up in the middle of the previous stitch. Repeat.

Satin stitch

1 This is often used to fill in a shape, so you could start by marking the outline of the shape on the fabric. Bring the needle up through the fabric at your starting point, usually at the end of the narrowest point of the shape.

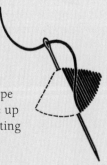

2 Insert the needle on the opposite side of the shape you are filling to make the first stitch. Take the next stitch right next to the first – you are aiming to fill the shape with solid colour.

3 Come up and go down through the outline of the shape each time, making your stitches longer or shorter as necessary. Take care that you don't pull the stitches too tight or it will pull the fabric in and cause puckering.

Chain stitch

1 Come up through the fabric at the end of the chain you wish to stitch. Take the needle back down through the fabric right next to where you came out, then bring it out a chain-length away, but don't pull the needle through. Wrap the thread under the tip of the needle.

2 Pull the thread through to form the first loop of the chain. To make the next chain, go back down inside the loop, right next to where the thread comes out, take a chain length stitch and wrap the thread under the needle.

3 Continue in this way, until the length of chain is as long as you like. To finish, take a small stitch over the end of the final chain to secure it and fasten off in the usual way.

Couching

1 This technique uses two threads, one that is laid down on the surface and one that is stitched over it to hold it down. You can use two different colour threads, or two the same colour.

Bring the first thread up through the fabric and lay it along the surface in a straight horizontal line.

2 Bring the second thread up through the fabric just below the line of the laid thread and take a tiny vertical whip stitch (see page 19) over the top. Repeat along the laid thread.

3 At the end of the line take a tiny horizontal stitch and curve the laid thread around it to run back on top of itself. Make small whip stitches to hold the second line of laid thread down.

4 On the second and subsequent lines, offset whip stitches between the stitches of the row below.

Stem stitch

1 This has the appearance of two threads that are twisted together, perfect for creating solid linear elements and outlines that have a textured quality. Bring your needle up from the back and make a first stitch slightly longer than usual. With the needle underneath, move the point back and bring it up at the midpoint of the previous stitch.

2 Make the next stitch a bit shorter than the first. Before pulling your thread taut and with the needle underneath again, bring the needle up back at the point where the previous stitch ends.

3 Pull the needle up and the thread taut before moving forward again with the next stitch. Repeat. For a consistent twisted look make sure the needle comes up on the same side of the previous stitch every time.

needle felting

Needle felting is a technique for creating felt objects without the use of water, but on a smaller scale it is also a perfect mending technique on wool garments and fabric. Felting is usually done with roving wool, the raw fleece before it is spun, which is available in a wide range of colours, but you can experiment with other fibres to see what works. You will also need a specialized needle, which is longer than a normal needle and has a shaft with several tiny barb-like protrusions, and a surface to work on – I use a dense sponge or piece of foam so that the needle has something soft to go into and doesn't get damaged.

1 Place the foam sponge underneath the area or hole that you want to needle felt, and place a bit of wool roving on top. Use the needle to repeatedly poke the roving into and around the hole. This not only fills in the void but tangles up the fibres of fleece into a more solid fabric and bonds it to the wool fibres of the fabric that you are mending – as you push the needle in, the barbs grasp onto the fibres and push them together and into the fabric.

2 Work over the entire surface of the roving, using the tip of the needle to gather and move the roving into empty areas if need be. The more you poke the needle up and down into the wool, the denser it becomes, essentially becoming felt and locking into position. The idea is to create a dense shape that evenly fills the area with roving so that there are no bald spots and the surface will have a solid unified shape.

3 Needle felting is also a means of adding yarn as a decorative shape or form on the surface of a wool fabric, without there being a hole to mend. Choose some colourful roving for this – or if you want the mend to be visible and stand out in an interesting way.

NEEDLE FELTING

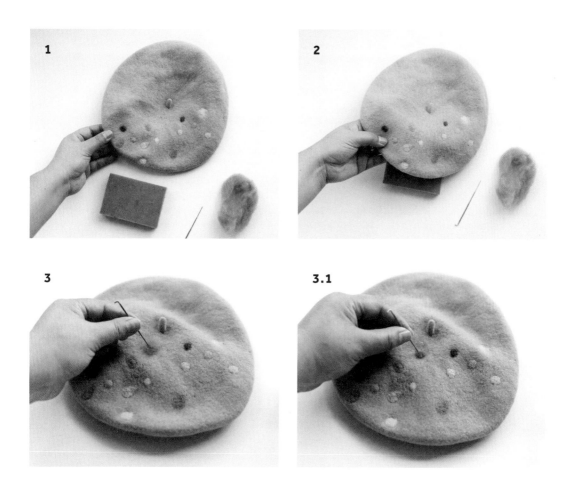

dyeing

Natural dyes offer amazing opportunities when looking to update or modify a garment. Not only is dyeing the perfect way to return faded items to their former appearance, but also to completely change the look and feel of a piece. Dyed clothes and household fabrics can also be combined with other materials to make entirely new items, such as dyeing old bed sheets and using that cloth to make a quilt.

While it's true that some natural dyes can give bright colours, the typical colours tend to be more subdued. The types of colours derived from many common plant or vegetable dyes tend to be more earthy tones, which while a little duller, have a timeless beauty with a range of shades and tones that evoke an almost emotional response. What is great is that sources for natural dyes, especially the plant-based ones, are all around us – essentially anything you can boil. But there are always surprises; not all work the way you might think, and they can fade over time and with light. But it's all worth it because there is nothing like naturally-dyed fabric.

Before you begin there are a few things you need to think about. Dyeing in general – and natural dyeing specifically – is a broad subject and can be quite complex, so it is not always easy to set out general rules and there are always exceptions and variations. But it doesn't always have to be complex, and there are many ways to explore these techniques at home or in your studio.

Typically there are only a few items you will need: the fabric, the dyestuff (the natural ingredients that are the dyes) and the dyebath (the dyestuff mixed with water and some additives to aid in the process). The type of fabric you want to dye is important because the dye needs to interact with the specific fibres on a molecular level. Animal fibre-based fabrics such as wool and silk are protein, whereas plant-based fabrics such as cotton and linen are cellulose. The difference is in how they receive the colour and whether you need to add any additives such as a mordant. It's difficult to generalize here because although cellulose fibres tend to need a mordant – which helps the dye bind with the fibres of the fabric – many dyers also use a mordant on fibres such as wool to increase colour intensity and to help the colour last. There are many mordants, and some work better than others for specific types of cloth and dyestuff, but two common ones are tannin and alum. Depending on the recipe, mordants can be added before, during or after the dyeing process, but for most situations the fabric is soaked in the mordant prior to dyeing. Some dyestuffs already contain tannins within them, but many do not and rely on a mordant being used to pre-treat the fibres prior to the dyeing process. The instructions here cover the basic process, but you would be well advised to follow recipes for specific materials and dyes, and to reference a natural dyeing book with detailed descriptions.

The list of dye ingredients capable of producing colour is seemingly endless. There are a lot of things from your kitchen that you can use to dye with; for example avocado pits give a lovely pink colour, onion skins result in a yellow colour, and purple cabbage gives a rich purple hue. And of course there is indigo, which is available through craft stores.

Natural dye process

1 There are a lot of different mordants that you can use but one that is used a lot is alum and it's a good safe one to use. Soak the cloth in alum for three hours before you dye the fabric.

2 There are a lot of formulas for the dyestuff, and the ratio of how much dyestuff you use to the weight of fabric will determine the depth of colour. I go by a simple method of using an equal weight of dyestuff to the weight of the fabric I am dyeing.

3 Boil your dyestuff for a few hours on a medium to high heat. Allow the dye bath to cool down slightly, removing any small bits of debris. Take your cloth from the alum bath and put it in the dye bath, then slowly start to raise the temperature.

4 You should be able to see the colour immediately on the fabric. After the dyebath has come to a simmer, let it sit for one hour to cool down again.

5 Once the dyebath cools down remove your fabric, rinse and hang to dry. Keep in mind the fabric will look darker when it's wet and will usually go lighter in colour once it is dry.

Dyeing with indigo

1 Dyeing with indigo is a little different than other natural dyes in that indigo is a vat dye, which means you don't need to boil it so it is much easier to use. There are a lot of recipes that you can use for dyeing with indigo, but I find using a pre-reduced indigo kit works well. The dye will come in three parts: indigo dye, thorea dioxide and sodium carbonate (bicarbonate of soda/baking soda). Follow the kit instructions to make the dye vat and let it sit tightly covered in a warm place overnight. The vat is ready after it 'flowers', which is when a foam-like shape has formed in the centre.

2 You are now ready to dye. Indigo dye is kind of magical; the vat will be a greenish colour. Wet your fabric with water and squeeze out any excess. Wearing gloves, dip your fabric into the vat for a moment and then pull out. When you pull your fabric out of the vat you will notice the colour change from green to a blue as it reacts with oxygen.

3 The colour on your fabric won't get stronger by keeping it longer in the vat. To get a darker blue dip the cloth multiple times, or as many times as you need, allowing it to turn blue between each dip. This is how I was able to achieve different tones of blue for the indigo quilt project (see page 138).

4 Once you are happy with the colour, rinse the fabric and hang it to dry. Keep in mind the fabric will look darker when it's wet and will usually go lighter in colour once it is dry.

printing

One of the oldest forms of printing is by using carved blocks with a raised surface design, which you roll ink onto and then push onto a cloth. One of the easiest things you can use to create a block is to carve into a potato, but you can also use found objects from nature or around your house that will create a texture or print. I most often use soft linoleum, which comes in sheets with a texture like an eraser, and can be carved with a lino cutter carving tool. You will also need fabric ink, a small foam roller, and a tray or plate to roll the ink onto. Printing your own fabric will create a custom look and the fabric can be used to create patching and mending pieces, or to make larger items in your home such as pillows and quilts. This is also a fun way to give an old garment a new life.

1 Before starting make sure the fabric you are printing on has been washed and dried. This will help the ink permeate the surface.

2 Draw your design onto the block with a pencil, bearing in mind that when you print the image will be reversed. Indicate which parts you don't want to be inked – these are the parts that will need to be removed. Now carefully carve these areas away. You want to carve deep enough so

that the ink doesn't get into the grooves and make unwanted marks.

3 Pour some fabric ink into the plate and spread it out with the foam roller. Roll a generous amount of ink over the block until all areas are inked, but not too thick. Take the block and lay it carefully on the cloth, pushing downward with your fingers but taking care not to accidentally move the block. Be sure to press with your fingers all over the surface so that it prints evenly.

4 Lift the block away cleanly. If there are some areas that you missed it's okay because this gives it a handmade look and the imperfections provide character. Carry on in this way until you have printed over the area.

5 Once you are done printing, leave the fabric to fully dry. Cover with an old pillowcase or spare piece of fabric and then run a hot iron over the front and back for two to three minutes on high heat with no steam. This is called heat setting and it prevents the ink from washing off in the laundry. If it's a large piece, you can put it in the dryer for ten minutes on a high heat.

finishing and tying knots

For a lot of the mending I do on knitwear I try not to create knots in the mending yarn because they might be felt when you are wearing the garment. Instead, what I normally do is to leave a tail about 7.5cm (3in) long at the start and end of the mend, and then weave them into the back of the piece.

TAILOR'S KNOT

This knot is used at the start of a mend. When cutting your length of thread, you want it to always be an arm's length and no longer.

1 You will need a threaded needle. Take the long tail and place it over the needle, so the end protrudes over the needle slightly. Hold the end in place with the hand holding the needle.

2 Wrap the thread around the needle several times – how many times determines how big the knot will be. Pinch the wraps together with finger and thumb.

3 While still pinching the wrapped threads, push them toward the eye of the needle. When you get to the eye of the needle, gently release your grip slightly and carry on pulling until you reach the bottom of the thread. What you are doing is pulling the knot and needle away from each other in opposite directions.

4 Snip the thread tail down to 5mm (¼in).

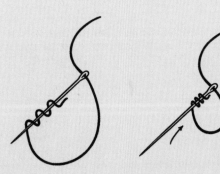
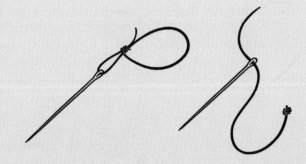

FINISHING KNOT

This is used at the end of a piece of hand sewing, after you have taken the needle through to the back of the fabric.

1 Turn the fabric over so you are looking at the reverse.

2 Take your needle under the previous stitch and pull the thread until a loop forms.

3 Pass the needle through the loop and pull until a knot is formed. To secure the end further by creating a larger knot, repeat steps 2 and 3.

4 Snip the thread tail down to 5mm (¼in).

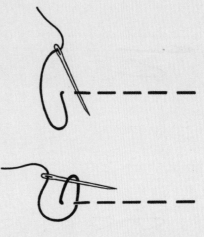

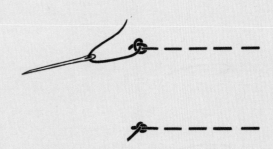

mending
by hand

Hand sewing is the most enjoyable process
for me; it makes me feel very connected to the
piece I am working on. Stitch by stitch, with
slight imperfections showing the evidence of my
handiwork – it's a meditative process that is both
creative and emotionally satisfying.

PROJECTS

PROJECT REPAIR

jeans

There's probably no garment in your wardrobe that doesn't age better than a pair of denim jeans. In fact for jeans ageing isn't a negative – it's a desired look. There's also no item in your wardrobe that is more loved; they are not precious, but yet you have a real physical connection with them. Jeans material is tough and can be heavily worn yet it is perfectly suitable for mending no matter what condition it is in. The most worn areas are the knees and pockets, which gives you lots of room to experiment and to combine different mending techniques. The blue jeans in this project had five areas that needed mending so I decided to do a variety of patching and appliqué combined with sashiko stitching. You could certainly stick with just one method if you choose, but I thought it would make it interesting to have a variety of areas on one pair of jeans that created a composition when viewed all together.

tools and materials

Pair of jeans or similar item

Denim and remnant fabric pieces

Fabric scissors

Thread snips

Pins

Sewing needle and thread

Sashiko needle

Sashiko threads in blue and white

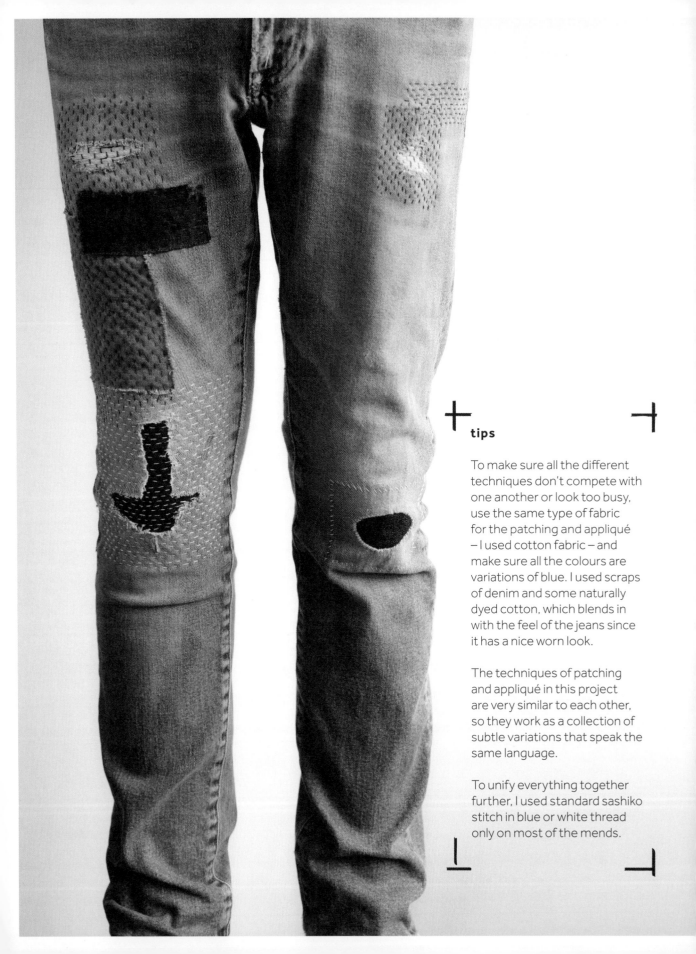

tips

To make sure all the different techniques don't compete with one another or look too busy, use the same type of fabric for the patching and appliqué – I used cotton fabric – and make sure all the colours are variations of blue. I used scraps of denim and some naturally dyed cotton, which blends in with the feel of the jeans since it has a nice worn look.

The techniques of patching and appliqué in this project are very similar to each other, so they work as a collection of subtle variations that speak the same language.

To unify everything together further, I used standard sashiko stitch in blue or white thread only on most of the mends.

1 Both knees were worn with open holes that needed to be mended, but because knees are high-wear areas it's a good idea to reinforce the entire area as well. Both were mended with simple patching underneath using a scrap of denim on the back of each hole, but rather than do identical techniques on both I gave one hole a clean edge with a regular oval shape, while on the other I let the ragged shape of the hole remain visible. I also used different sewing stitches on each knee.

2 For the clean-edged hole, first clean around the hole to give it the desired shape and to remove any loose threads. It's a good idea to cut the stitching on the inside leg seam – to open the leg up – this will allow you to get your hands underneath the fabric easily. Turn the leg inside out and stitch up the seam afterwards when all the work is done.

3 Cut a piece of fabric about 2.5cm (1in) larger than the hole all round. Place the fabric underneath, centred on the hole, and pin in place. Fold under the raw edge of the hole by about 5mm (¼in) to form a hem. Working from the right side, sew all around the hole with whip stitch (see page 19) to hold the edge of the hole to the appliqué patch beneath. I like to keep my stitches quite small and closely spaced.

4 Now turn the leg inside out to work on the inside. Using a slightly larger whip stitch, sew all around the loose edge of the fabric to attach it to the wrong side of the jeans.

5 On the other knee, clean up the edges of the hole just to remove any loose threads but keep the existing shape of the hole. Cut a piece of fabric the full width of the leg plus about 2.5cm (1in) all round. Centre underneath the hole and pin in place. On this side I kept the raw edges of the hole and secured the layers by creating a field of sashiko stitches (see page 43) in white thread. Support the layers of fabric with one hand, making

sure there are no buckles or wrinkles, then start your running stitch in one corner and continue, back and forth until the entire fabric is covered. Secure with a finishing knot (see page 57).

6 The areas beneath the pockets were also worn with holes, but in both cases the white threads of the warp still remained adding yet another level of detail to the fabric. Because of this I left the edges raw and just carefully trimmed any loose threads.

7 For the left pocket cut piece of scrap fabric a little larger than the hole and secure it underneath the hole with pins. Work sashiko stitching in blue to contrast with the white of the threads, running up and down until the entire patch underneath is sewn to the jeans fabric.

8 Over the hole I carefully went over and under the exposed threads as I sewed the sashiko stitching, so that it looked like it was woven. One side looked like it could use a few more stitches, so I switched direction and overlapped them in that area just for visual impact.

9 The hole beneath the right pocket needed a bit more work, because it had a large area of thin fabric below it down the front of the jeans. I treated the hole itself in the same way as for the left pocket, so repeat steps 7 and 8.

10 To deal with the thin area of fabric beneath, cut a couple of rectangular patches – these can be in different fabrics for extra interest: one of my patches was dyed with indigo (see page 53).

11 Place the two patches on the front of the jeans and pin in place, one horizontal and one vertical. Use sashiko stitching in blue thread to secure all the layers. I continued the running stitches in blue down the entire front, so they slight overlapped the white sashiko stitches of the knee mend.

PROJECT REPAIR

butterfly appliqué

It's always disappointing to pull a sweater or shirt out from storage only to find that moths have found the piece irresistible. What better way to mend the damage than to appliqué some adorable little moths, or perhaps butterflies, over the holes and reclaim your wardrobe. Using appliqué to repair a hole is similar to the idea of patching; the difference is that with appliqué you're creating an image, making the patch pictorial. There are so many possibilities for appliqué to save and redefine any garment by adding motifs, patterns or images, and embroidery is the perfect companion to add colour and detail. Even if there is no damage to speak of, using images and needlework can transform any piece into something special.

tools and materials

Garment to be repaired

Tracing paper and pencil

Thin card

General-purpose scissors

Water-soluble fabric pencil

Small piece of remnant fabric, such as natural dye linen

Fabric scissors

Pins

Sewing needle and thread

Thread snips

Stranded embroidery thread (floss)

Embroidery needle

Embroidery hoop (optional)

1 Use the template on page 149 for the butterfly images or create your own. You may need to increase or decrease the template size to ensure sure that it is slightly larger than the hole you are covering. Copy the different shapes of the image onto the card and cut them out.

2 Using the water-soluble pencil, draw around the template shapes onto your remnant fabric and cut the shapes out, giving them an additional 5mm (¼in) seam allowance all around. Place the shapes right side up over your hole to make up the butterfly, and pin in place.

3 There are a number of stitches that you can use to hold the appliqué in place but I used a slip stitch (see page 41). On one end bring your needle up through all the layers and make a double stitch to start. Folding under the seam allowance as you work, continue slip stitching around the shape, placing stitches about 3mm (⅛in) apart, until the shape is attached.

4 If you feel there's too much bulk in the fabric as you fold the edges under, especially at corners or points, you can snip a bit away from the seam allowance. When you are working with curves it's a good idea to snip into the seam allowance at the curve, so when you turn your fabric under it creates a nice arch.

5 After you finish one shape, repeat with the others until your butterfly appliqué is complete, ending with a finishing knot (see page 57) each time. If you are adding more butterfly appliqués, finish them all before moving onto the embroidery details.

6 Choose some embroidery thread (floss) that will contrast with the fabric below and begin stitching the embroidery to create the details as shown on the template image. I used backstitch for the linear elements, such as the butterfly antenna and wing details; running stitch for the little dashes on the wings; and satin stitch for the body and triangle design on the wings (see pages 16–20 for embroidery stitches). Vary the colours, textures and shapes to give each butterfly a distinct appearance.

7 When you have finished give the appliqué a light pressing.

tips

A cereal box is ideal for the thin card that you need for the template shapes. Don't cut it with your fabric scissors or thread snips, as that will blunt hem – use ordinary household scissors.

The lines made by a water-soluble pencil will vanish when sprayed with water, but it's probably a good idea to test this on a spare scrap of the fabric before you begin as the ink can react with some fabrics and become permanent. You could also use an air-soluble pencil, which makes lines that just fade away over time.

PROJECT REPAIR

sweater

We all have sweaters hiding in our closets that are well loved but may have developed wear holes on places like elbows, or perhaps a random little hole from moths. The technique that I chose for this piece is a darning weave, and the great thing about this type of visible mending is that you can use yarn to make a weave within the knit to fill the hole, rather than simply covering it over with a patch. I like that this allows you to be expressive with the yarn that you choose, so that it stands out through colour, pattern, texture and the shape of the mend. So not only are you repairing the sweater for use, but adding a design element as well. No matter what sweater you start with, it will speak of the handmade and be a piece you are proud to wear again.

tools and materials

Knitted sweater or similar item

Thread snips

Darning mushroom or glass jar (optional)

Elastic band

2 colours of yarn in similar weight and same material as the sweater

Tapestry needle no. 12

Scissors

Elastic bands to hold the sweater in place

tips

There really isn't a right or wrong choice or yarn for this project – you can weave with many different weights of yarn or types of thread – but with some types of material you will get different results. I wanted the darn to have a unified look and feel to the original garment, and just let the colour and the appearance of the stitches stand out. For this reason I used DMC tapestry wool, which was a similar weight to the yarn of the sweater. I chose two different colours, one for the vertical (warp) and the other for the horizontal (weft).

I don't like to create knots so when I begin weaving I leave a tail that I can weave in (see page 26) after I am done.

When weaving over and under do not tug too hard on the yarn as this will create too much tension in the weave – it will pucker and may cause the sweater to be smaller in that area, making it uncomfortable to wear. Give it a bit of slack, so that when you are done the weave will stay flat.

1 Before beginning, make sure to clean the edge of the hole. If there are any loose threads or if it's an odd shape it might be best to clean it up a bit with some snips.

2 To make it easier to start, I would put an object in the sleeve so that you have a surface to work on. A wooden darning mushroom is best, but something like a glass jar that you can slide down the sleeve works too. Centre the hole to be mended against the surface and use an elastic band around the sweater so that it's secured on the object.

3 Begin with the warp threads, so decide which colour you want to use first. Starting roughly 2.5cm (1in) from the outside of the hole (your starting point is up to you; it can be further from the hole if you'd like to create a larger mend, or closer), bring the yarn through from inside the sweater leaving a yarn tail of about 7.5cm (3in) on the inside. Begin a running stitch (see page 16) within the existing knit of the sweater, with a stitch length of about 5mm (¼in) and stitching toward the open hole. If the sweater is thicker make longer stitches; if it is thinner you might want to make your stitches smaller – this doesn't affect the mend, it's more for aesthetics.

4 As your running stitch reaches the hole, leave a length of yarn across the opening – the length you are leaving is the part you will be weaving – and then continue the running stitch on the opposite side of the hole for about 2.5cm (1in). Repeat this process back and forth over the hole until it is covered, keeping the stitch rows close to each other. As you did at the start, leave a yarn tail of about 7.5cm (3in) on the inside of the sweater.

You can also mend a sweater using blanket stitch. The threads of a blanket stitch don't extend into the existing fabric, which can be very effective if you want to emphasize the mend through shape, colour and texture. See page 31 for further instructions on how to create this stitch.

5 Now create the weft with the other colour, working 90 degrees from the previous running stitch. As before, start about 2.5cm (1in) from the edge of the hole, leave a tail of yarn about 7.5cm (3in) on the inside, and work a running stitch toward the hole. When you reach the hole, weave your darning needle under and over all the warp threads that you created previously. Repeat this on each row, back and forth, working the opposite over and under on each row to build up a woven patch over the hole.

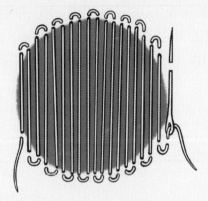

6 If you run out of yarn, finish the old yarn and start the new one with tails of about 7.5cm (3in) on the inside of the sweater.

7 Once you have finished it's good to give that area a light steam to flatten and even out any puckered areas. Weave in the tails of the yarns.

8 This sweater had two wear holes on the sleeve so I repeated this process to mend the second hole. To change the look of each mend you can change or alternate the colours so the mends seem a little different from each other. You can also work your running stitches over a larger or smaller area of mending, extending some or all stitches as far as you wish, or modify the outer shape of the mend. Darn any other holes elsewhere on the garment in the same way.

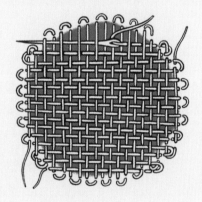

PROJECT REPAIR

socks

Socks are one thing that people go through a lot of; they are probably one of the most disposable items we wear. There was a time when handmade socks were precious because of the time involved in making them, so mending them helped to prolong their use. In today's world it's worth mending both the handmade and the machine-made ones. Worn areas are usually mostly on the heels, feet pads and toes. Mending can not only repair a hole – it can elevate a plain pair to another level of interest by adding colour and shape.

tools and materials

Pair of socks

Thread snips

Darning mushroom or tennis ball or light bulb

Elastic band

2ply (fingering) weight sock yarn (preferably the same material as the sock)

Tapestry needle

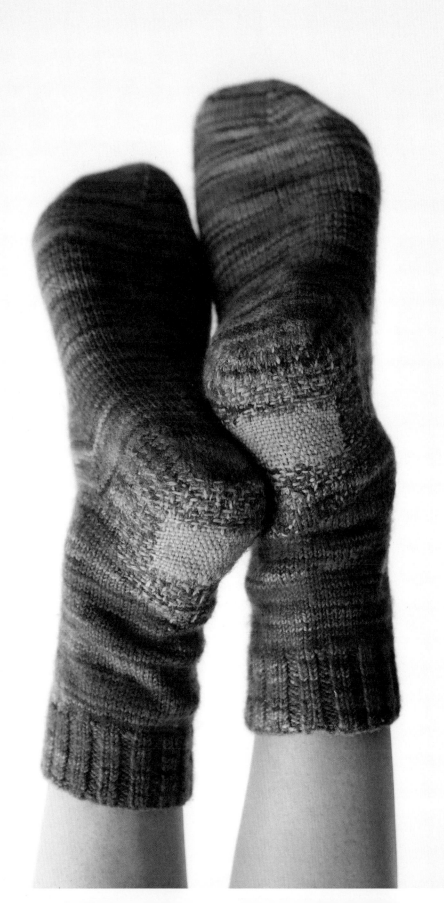

1 Before beginning, clean the edge of the hole. If there are any loose threads or if it's an odd shape it might be best to clean it up a bit with some snips. I decided to use the darning weave (see page 25), but you may decide that duplicate stitch (see page 30) or the blanket stitch darn (see page 31) would be better for your mend.

2 To make it easier to work, put the darning mushroom or a suitable substitute inside the sock so that you have a surface to work on. Centre the hole to be mended against the surface and use an elastic band around the sock so that it's secured on the mushroom.

3 Decide which colour yarn you want to use for the warp threads and thread the darning needle. Leaving a 7.5cm (3in) or so tail that you will later weave into the back, bring the needle through to the front about 2.5cm (1in) away from the edge of the hole. Work the darning weave as explained on page 26.

4 I tend to make my stitches about 5mm (¼in) long as I work toward the hole, but if the sock is thicker make longer stitch lengths and if the sock is thinner you might want to make your stitches smaller. The stitch length doesn't affect the mend – it's more for aesthetics.

5 Create the weft with another length of yarn, working at 90 degrees from the previous running stitch. When you reach the area where the hole is, take your darning needle under and over the warp threads to create a woven section. On the way back, go over where you went under, and vice versa, and continue to alternate on subsequent rows of stitching.

6 When weaving do not to tug too hard on the yarn because this will create too much tension in the weave. Allow a bit of slack – after the first wash the surface will even out with the rest of the sock.

7 Finish off with a 7.5cm (3in) or so tail. Turn the sock inside out and weave both tails into the back of the sock fabric.

tips

Choosing the right material for the mend is a good starting point. I like to use the same fibre as the sock, so if it's a wool sock use wool yarn to repair it. By using the same type of fibre, when the socks are washed the mend will not pucker up or shrink.

To change the look of each mend you can use different colours for the warp and the weft. You can also lengthen your running stitches to make larger or smaller areas of mending, or extend some or all of stitches further into the surrounding fabric for a different look or to modify the shape of the mend.

PROJECT REPAIR

mitts with duplicate stitch

Mittens that begin to wear thin are a common problem for those of us who live in northern countries and it's a shame to say goodbye to a pair that you've grown attached to. But the truth is that repairing wear and tear in any knitwear is much less daunting that you'd think, even for those of us with little or no knitting skills. This pair had thin areas but no holes yet, so were perfect for some duplicate stitch (see page 30), also known as Swiss darning, where you work over thin areas by stitching onto the existing fabric, mimicking the existing knitted stitch. Rather than hide my handiwork I used different coloured yarns to create a little freeform geometric pattern that almost appears as a patchwork. I wanted my repair to fit into the existing knit of the mittens as seamlessly as possible but stand out through colour and shape so as almost to look like an intentional part of the design. Because knitwear is structured in rows both horizontally and vertically I decided to stitch multi-coloured squares, playing with the placement of the colours in each area so it would appear as if the shapes were overlapping. There were three areas that needed mending and approaching each area in a similar way would make it seem like there was a larger pattern at play.

tools and materials

Pair of mitts or similar knitted item

Tapestry needle

Tapestry wool in various colours in a slightly lighter weight than the garment's original yarn

Thread snips

Darning egg (optional)

1 I tend to begin stitching from right to left and then upward, so I chose a spot just to the right and below the worn area to begin. Thread your needle with one of your colours and bring the needle from the inside of the mitts to the front through the middle of an existing stitch so that it appears at the bottom of a 'V', leaving a tail 5–7.5cm (2–3in) long on the inside, which you will weave into your work on the back afterward.

2 Follow the existing loop up and insert the needle from right to left underneath the two threads of the stitch in the row above. Pull the yarn through, and insert it back down into the spot where you started. You have just mimicked an existing knitted stitch and this will be the basic stitch you will use to create rows to fill in all the worn areas.

3 Bring the needle up at the bottom of the next 'V' in the stitch to the left, follow the loop up and insert your needle under the two threads of the stitch above, then take it back to the bottom of the 'V' again. Repeat along this row until you have gone beyond the worn area as far as you wish.

4 Now move up to the row above and continue stitching, this time working from left to right. I took care to stop and start each row directly on top of the row below, so that my rows were neat and the shapes appeared as squares.

5 When you have finished part of the worn area with one colour, switch colours and repeat the stitch and rows to create another little square. Shift your starting point for each area so that the squares appear independent of each other as if overlapping.

6 I placed a couple of rows in a lighter highlight colour on top of the last coloured square for visual interest.

7 When all the worn areas have been filled and you are happy with your design, turn the item inside out and tidy up all the loose ends by weaving them into the existing knit.

tips

You can only really work duplicate stitch over the 'V' stitches of stocking (stockinette) stitch fabric, although you could use other embroidery stitches to both mend and create a pattern on other types of knitted fabric.

You could sketch out your design on graph paper before you begin, with each square equalling one stitch.

PROJECT REPAIR

blazer

The wool twill blazer is a classic and it's a piece in your wardrobe that you will want to take care of and hang onto. Wool blazers like this are prone to moths, which can leave arbitrary holes where you would least expect them. Such damage might be annoying, but wool coats offer an excellent opportunity to be really creative – and the addition of some visible mending can uplift any jacket into a really stylish one. There are a number of techniques that would be great in this situation, such as reverse appliqué, but I found some wool remnants and a few small wool samples that looked perfect for the job. They had a colour palette that suited the blue-greys of the jacket and the textures and weights worked as well. Fortunately the majority of the wear and holes were on the front near the buttons, which is a great place for some decorative work, so I created a patchwork along either side of the front. The other great thing about patchwork is that you don't have to deconstruct any of the blazer, simply sew on top.

tools and materials

Wool jacket or similar item

Remnants or small pieces of wool fabric

Fabric scissors

Sewing pins (optional)

Sashiko thread

Sashiko needle

1 Lay the jacket flat on your table and arrange your fabric pieces on top. There are no clear rules to dictate your placement – just arrange them to cover up any wear or moth holes and to create a nice composition. Feel free to overlap pieces to emphasize the patchwork nature of the mend.

2 Trim any pieces that seem too large so that they work as a nice addition to the jacket without overpowering it. For instance you could trim the occasional piece so that it reflects the shape of one or two of the original pockets. Find a balance so that your pieces fit in with the jacket as well as acting as a patch; for this reason I kept the darkest fabric to a minimum so it didn't seem too heavy.

3 Once you are happy with your arrangement and any pieces that need to be cut are trimmed, do a quick sketch or take a photo with your phone. You'll have to move all the pieces because you will be sewing each piece on separately, so you need to remember where each piece goes.

4 Remove any buttons that may be affected by the patchwork and put them aside, to be replaced later.

5 I wanted to wrap the fabric patches around the jacket edge in some places to give a nice structured edge – and since the pieces I was using didn't fray I didn't have to tuck under their edges, which would have caused extra bulk. Place the fabric piece along the edge inside the jacket and with right sides together. Work a line of running stitch (see page 16) about 5mm (¼in) from the edge. Flip the fabric over the edge and wrap it around, pulling it tight. Hold the fabric in place with whip stitch (see page 19) around the edge. Repeat on any other pieces that will wrap around.

6 Then, starting with the lower layers, begin attaching the other fabric pieces to the jacket front using whip stitch around the entire edge of each piece. I chose to use a white sashiko thread as a nice balance, so the thread would be noticeable but not too decorative. You can use regular thread instead but the sashiko thread is a little heavier.

7 Be sure you only sew through the outer layer of the jacket and not through to the lining, or accidentally into a pocket. Carry on adding pieces until your design is complete.

8 To finish, sew the buttons back on (see page 21) in their original places. If you have covered up any buttonholes, as I did, you will also have to cut a new hole and finish the raw edges with a buttonhole stitch (see page 20).

tip

Try to keep a balance of pieces on each side of the jacket front, but don't make it completely symmetrical – have a few more on one side, and perhaps some smaller pieces further up on the lapel on one side.

PROJECT REPAIR

button shirt

A shirt like this is a staple in your wardrobe – usually it's made from fine cotton or linen and through use it tends to wear at the cuff, elbows, collars and bottom edge. The mending on the edge of this garment adds an unexpected detail that creates an interesting visual surprise on an otherwise plain shirt. For this piece I wanted to use a fine cotton that was similar in weight to the shirt and work patching on top and beneath, as well as reinforcing the surface of the really worn areas with sashiko stitches; the added layer underneath makes the cloth much stronger. I used the holes as a road map to guide my mend, which I think creates a lovely pattern with strong shapes – while the sashiko stitches give the shirt interesting texture.

tools and materials

Plain cotton/linen shirt or similar item

Thread snips

Fabric scissors

Pieces of fabric

Sewing needle and thread

Safety pins (optional)

Cotton embroidery thread (floss)

Embroidery hoop (optional)

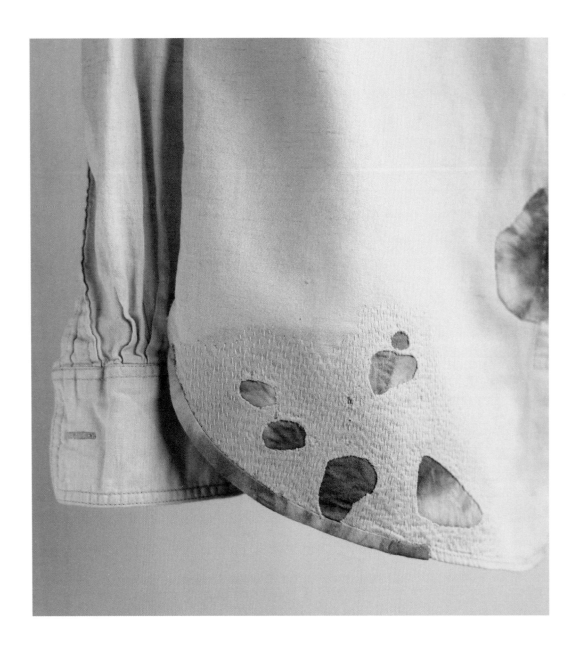

1 Before beginning make sure to clean up the holes by carefully clipping away any loose threads.

2 Start by doing the patching beneath (see page 36). After securing the patch fabric behind the holes, fold under the top fabric around the edge of each hole by 5mm (¼in). Sew the top fabric to the patch fabric all around each hole using slip stitch or blanket stitch (see pages 19 and 20) using sewing thread.

3 When you have finished, press the fabric with an iron.

4 Now using cotton embroidery thread (floss), work lines of running stitch in the areas around the patch, making sure to sew through both layers. The running stitch not only holds the layers together but also gives the shirt a bit more body and makes it more durable.

5 Remove the button and cover the hole at the middle front of the shirt with an applied patch (see page 34). You can choose to leave the edges raw and work sashiko stitching (see page 43) over the surface, or you can fold under the raw edges and slip stitch along the edge. I worked a line of running stitch in cotton embroidery thread (floss) across the patch, following the line of the stitching on the button band area, giving it some detail and also securing the fabric down. Replace the button in its original position.

6 The bottom edge of the shirt was torn so I replaced it by add a binding (see page 32) in the patch fabric, which emphasized the edge of the shirt and gave it a nice linear element.

tips

I chose a shibori-dyed fabric that I already had, with areas of white that I liked and which gave the patch shapes a stone-like quality. Other fabrics you could try are patterned or plain quilting fabric, or try combining different fabrics in the same colour scheme. I used just one type of fabric to give the piece some unity.

I tend to not use pins to hold down fabric because I always stab myself, so instead I use a contrasting sewing thread and tack (baste) the fabric by doing large loose running stitches. Using safety pins is also a good alternative.

PROJECT REPAIR

beret

This project shows how a simple mend can completely reinvent a garment. In fact, if you didn't know there were holes, the mend would appear as an intentional design element! This wool beret was damaged with moth holes and I wanted to mend it with a material that was similar to the felt of the beret but still maintained the holes as visible elements. The key was to use needle felting so that I could minimize any difference in material, but use a range of bright colours that would still highlight the mend. And because of the random placement of the holes, the mend appears as a playful array of colour that was meant to be.

tools and materials

Wool beret

Dense sponge

Small bits of wool roving

Needle felting needle

1 The sponge gives you a small surface to work on and protects the surface or your fingers beneath, so place it underneath the area where you will be needle felting.

2 Pull off a pinch of the wool roving and place it on top of the area you want to mend. Using your needle, push down into the roving repeatedly, while gathering the roving so that it forms a circular shape. The point of the needle will safely extend into the sponge below.

3 Add more roving on top and keep on punching with the needle until you have built up the desired surface – the more roving you add, the darker and more opaque the colour will be. The felt you are creating will also be denser – I personally like it to be dense so that you don't see through to the surface below.

4 Continue working until the roving has solidified into felt and is securely attached as part of the beret fabric.

5 Repeat the steps on any other holes or surfaces of the beret to create different size circles using a variety of colours.

tip

Needle felting is a process in which you create a felted area by pushing wool roving into a surface or into a void, using a special needle that has small burrs along its length. It's a repetitive process that builds up the surface with dense interlocking fibres of wool. This technique can be used on other wool items like sweaters and other garments, so experiment to see its potential. You can also play around with the shapes that you make.

PROJECT RENEW

making felt patches

Adding a patch is the most basic form of mending and personally I like the simplicity of what a little spot of colour, texture or pattern can give to a garment or accessory. Here's an idea that will take the simple patch to another level – create your own patches with custom motifs, drawings or any form of artwork you can think of. I wanted to make a whole series of little images of the kinds of things I love to draw and paint: botanical things like leaves and branches, little moths and insects and a few small abstract shapes as well. I decided to use embroidery on wool felt to take advantage of the bright colours available in embroidery thread (floss). Embroidery is one of those types of needlework that grabs your attention no matter what the size, so you can pack a lot of lustre and detail into small areas. These embroidered patches are a great way to cover holes of any size. The wool felt backing is perfect for fine stitchwork; it won't fray and can be easily stitched or ironed onto any garment or accessory.

tools and materials

Fine dark permanent marker

Water-soluble transfer paper, such as stick 'n' stitch paper or magic paper

Water-soluble fabric pencil (optional)

Wool felt in various colours

Fabric scissors

Stranded embroidery thread (floss) in various colours

Embroidery needle

Thread snips

Double-sided fusible interfacing (optional)

1 Using the permanent marker, trace one of the templates on page 150, or your own design, onto the transfer paper. Peel the backing off the transfer paper and stick it to the felt. If you are drawing directly onto the felt, you will need to copy the image and then use a water-soluble fabric pencil to draw it onto the felt.

2 Because the felt is stiff, it doesn't need to be held in an embroidery hoop so you can work on each image individually if you prefer. If so, cut the felt backing into smaller pieces, making sure you leave enough room around the image to comfortably work with it in your hand – you will trim the patch to size afterward. However, if working on a hoop is more comfortable, then use a whole sheet of wool felt with multiple images drawn on it, spaced apart so that they can be cut and trimmed afterward.

3 While these projects are perfect for any embroidery stitches you like, I used only satin stitch (see page 47) and backstitch (see page 18). For linear elements use backstitch, and for solid shapes use a satin stitch to fill each area with a specific colour. Choose your colour of embroidery thread (floss) and separate out three strands to thread in the needle. Embroider each design in your chosen colours, following the lines on the transfer paper and working through it into the felt.

4 When you have finished the images trim the felt backing to shape, either by following the shape of the image or by giving it its own shape such as a square or oval. Leave at least 12mm (½in) around each image so that when you sew the patch down the edge stitching doesn't visually interfere with your images.

5 Run the patches one at a time under warm tap (faucet) water, while gently rubbing the water-soluble paper away with your fingers. When all the paper has dissolved, pat the area with a clean cloth and lay flat to dry.

6 If using a patch to mend a hole, place it over the hole and work whip stitch (see page 19) over the edge of the patch to attach it all around to the garment or fabric. You could also use any other embroidery stitch of your choice, or use double-sided fusible interfacing to iron the patch onto the item.

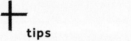

tips

You can enlarge or reduce the images provided on page 150, and they can also be used to decorate anything you like, such as a backpack or the lapel of a jacket.

Select a variety of colours for each design. Because the images are small, choose a combination of bright colours and a few darks for contrast.

For these embroideries I used water-soluble transfer paper, but you can draw directly onto the felt backing if it is light in colour.

PROJECT RENEW

embroidered dress

Everybody has more than enough of what we call 'basics' – those everyday garments that aren't meant to be anything special, let alone even noticeable, at least without an accessory. But, what if we treated these items as a blank canvas, using stitching techniques as a way to add detail and personality? Embroidery is the perfect way to turn something basic into something better. My daughter had this dress with fine black checks, which was lovely in its simplicity but was a little plain and definitely lacked her personality. I decided to embroider some floral imagery on the shoulders, which she loves so it now has a special place in her wardrobe.

tools and materials

Plain dress or similar item

Fine dark permanent marker

Water-soluble transfer paper, such as stick 'n' stitch or magic paper

18cm (7in) embroidery hoop

Stranded cotton embroidery thread (floss)

Embroidery needle no. 8

Thread snips

1 Using the templates on page 149, or your own design, decide where to place your embroidered image on your dress or shirt. I liked the flat panel on the shoulders of this dress and decided that would be a good spot to add some colourful details. I chose to hang the images upside down for a more unusual and less formal appearance and adjusted their scale to fit the location.

2 Once you have decided on your placement, use the permanent marker to trace the design onto the transfer paper. Cut around the image, peel off the backing and stick the transfer paper onto the area you want to embroider. Place your garment with the design centred in an embroidery hoop. You'll follow the lines on the transfer paper, embroidering through it into the fabric below.

3 Choose your colour of embroidery thread (floss) and separate out three strands to thread into the needle. When embroidering floral images I tend to start with the stem in backstitch (see page 18), placing the stitches close together so they build up to a nice width. I then use satin stitch (see page 47) for all solid areas, starting with the leaves, then the smaller stems and lastly the flowers. Use different colours or shades and change the direction of the stitches to highlight each shape. To provide more detail, depth and visual interest, use small single running stitches to overlay lines of colour on top of the petals of the small flowers.

4 Hold the embroidered areas one at a time under warm running water, while gently rubbing away the water-soluble paper with your fingers. When all the paper has dissolved, pat the area with a clean cloth and lay flat to dry.

tips

My design was done on water-soluble transfer paper, which made it really easy to move around until I found a playful location on either shoulder. It also made it easy to focus on the stitches while working, without any distraction from the patterned cloth below.

Cotton embroidery thread (floss) usually has six strands but I used only three strands for this project for finer detail. You can use all six if you prefer but that will make the image bulkier.

PROJECT RENEW

embroidery on mitts

Adding embroidery to an otherwise plain item is the perfect way to add details or a motif. These mittens were colourful but lacked anything else that would make them seem special. I love botanical imagery and I thought the bright yellow gave me a good canvas to showcase my flower drawing. The colours that I chose are simple but contrast with the bright background, so that the repeated shapes and flower form really stand out. For this project I used water-soluble transfer paper since it was difficult to draw the motif on the surface of the mitten because of its soft texture. Not only did this allow me to draw my motif and place it exactly where I wanted it, but made the embroidery easy as well since I just had to follow the drawn image.

tools and materials

Pair of mitts or similar item

Fine permanent marker

Water-soluble transfer paper such as stitch 'n' stick or magic paper

Tapestry needle no. 18

Wool tapestry yarn in dark green, light green, pale pink and red

Thread snips

1 Using the permanent marker, trace the template on page 151, or your own design, onto the transfer paper. Peel the backing off the transfer paper and stick it to the area of the mitt that you want to embroider.

2 Using the dark green yarn, embroider a line of backstitch (see page 18) through both the transfer paper and the mitten along the entire stem.

3 To fill in the leaves, work the bottom half of each leaf in satin stitch (see page 47), following the lines of the drawing and trying to keep your stitches parallel to each other on a slight angle so that they give an impression of veins. Switch to light green yarn and work the top half of each leaf in the same way, so that the stitches form a V shape.

4 Next work the flower. Using the pale pink yarn create long satin stitches between the centre point of the flower and the edge of each petal. Spread out the stitches so that they create a fan-shape petal. Finish all the pale pink areas and then work the alternate petals using red yarn.

5 Hold the mitts under warm running water, while gently rubbing the water-soluble paper away with your fingers. When all the paper has dissolved, pat the area with a clean cloth and lay flat to dry.

tips

You can use different coloured yarns to embroider the motif if you have mittens that are darker or lighter in colour.

When stitching, take care not to catch the underside of the mitt with your needle and tread.

PROJECT RENEW

block-printed sweatshirt

I do a lot of different kinds of printing and block printing is one of my favourite techniques. I love how accessible it is, that it uses very inexpensive materials, and how easy it is to do. The immediacy of this technique, in which you press the image onto the fabric, makes it instantly gratifying – and adding a print can transform an otherwise plain item into something special and unique. For this project I chose an old sweatshirt that needed some refreshing, so I drew an image of a leaf with a lovely shape that I could print across the entire front. By printing the same image I created a repeat pattern, but one without a strict overall plan – the design was placed at random, turning the block sometimes as I printed, giving the image a sense of movement. The versatility of block printing makes this technique great for experimentation, and the imperfections that result from printing on fabric make it a perfect expression of handmade.

tools and materials

Sweatshirt or similar item

Piece of soft linoleum slightly larger than image

3B pencil

White bond paper

Lino carving tool with interchangeable cutting nibs

Craft knife

Fabric ink

Plate for spreading the ink

Spatula

Small foam roller approx. 5cm (2in) wide, or a foam brush

Pillowcase or scrap fabric

Iron

HOW TO MAKE A BLOCK-PRINTED SWEATSHIRT

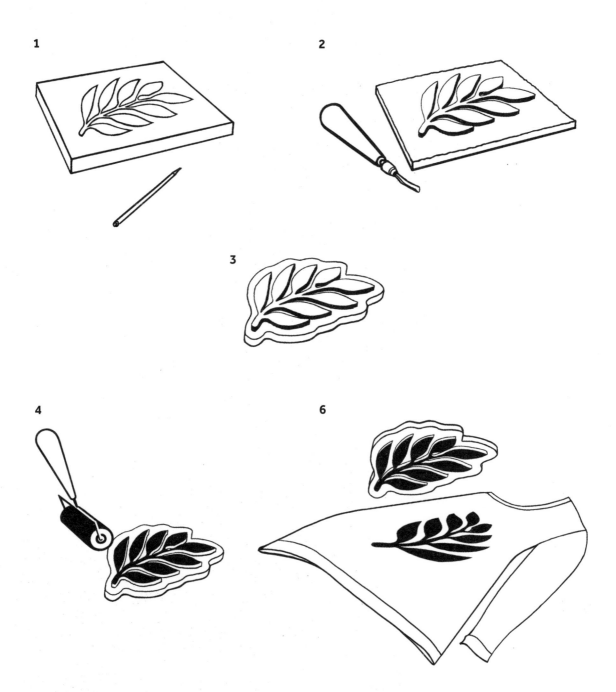

1 To transfer your image on the linoleum you can draw directly onto the block with a pencil or marker, or trace your design with carbon paper. My favourite method is to trace the outline of the block (see template on page 151) onto paper and then draw the image on the paper with a soft graphite pencil, making sure to colour in areas that I want to print. Place the block face down on the drawing and flip it over so that the back of your drawing is facing up. Using a soft pencil, draw or rub over the entire back of the drawing. This will transfer your drawing onto the surface of the block and will automatically reverse the image so the print will appear correctly – especially important if you have any text in the image.

2 Since you coloured in the areas you want to print, you need only remove the white areas of the block. Using the #3 cutting nib, and holding the block with one hand but away from the direction of the blade, remove the white areas by pushing the tool into the block deep enough that the tip of the tool almost disappears into the block. This will ensure that the cut away areas are not too shallow and will stay clear of unwanted ink during the printing process.

3 If there are any large areas to be cut away, remove these with the #5 cutting nib. Then clean up any details and edges with a craft knife, if necessary.

4 Pour some fabric ink onto the plate and spread it out with the spatula. Roll the foam roller over the ink until it is evenly covered. Roll the ink onto the block solidly, covering all raised areas with a generous amount of ink.

5 Make test prints on scrap fabric before you start printing to gauge how much ink and how much pressure you need. Keep in mind you will need to roll ink onto the block every time you do a print if you want a consistent depth of tone over the whole garment, otherwise subsequent prints will be quite faded. Alternatively, you can ink every other print if you would like to create different tones within the piece.

6 Place your first print anywhere on the garment. Press down firmly and don't move the block. Lift it up cleanly in one motion. Keep inking and printing, rotating the block at various degrees each time so that the image appears randomly placed.

7 Once you've printed as much as you wish, let the ink dry thoroughly. Place an old pillowcase or a piece of scrap fabric on top of the printed area and heat set the ink by pressing with an iron over the front and back of the garment using a high heat with no steam. This last step will make the ink permanent so it won't wash out in the laundry.

tips

To make the printing block I used soft linoleum, which is easy to carve a pattern into and can be reused over and over. Alternatively you can use a potato, or found objects with a texture, or even scrap materials like foam food trays or cardboard that can be cut into shapes and made into a block.

I use a Speedball cutting tool with interchangeable cutting nibs; I mostly use the #3 and #5 nibs.

PROJECT REUSE

sashiko stitch and patch sewing booklet

I almost always have a little needlework project within reach that I can pick up to make a few stitches whenever I have a quiet moment. Part of my sewing kit is this little booklet with felt pages and pockets that hold needles, scissors, threads, scrap fabric and little things like safety pins – everything I need to carry for a sewing project in fact. I make these booklets all the time with covers that are always different with interesting compositions. They are quick to make and are perfect to use up any remnant fabric you may have. For this version I used some indigo-dyed fabric combined with some small bits of printed fabric, with the addition of some sashiko stitches for extra detail – but anything you have on hand will be perfect. It is easy to adjust the booklet for the different items you carry and it also works nicely as a travel pouch for your jewellery.

tools and materials

Water-soluble fabric pencil

Approx. 14 x 20cm (5½ x 8in) of indigo or dark fabric

Sashiko needle

White sashiko thread

Remnant fabric in a mix of colours to make patchwork 2.5 x 14cm (1 x 5½in)

Fabric scissors

Sewing machine, or sewing needle and thread

10 x 25.5cm (4 x 10 in) of cotton muslin or any lightweight cotton for interior pocket

14 x 25.5cm (5½ x 10in) of cotton muslin or any lightweight cotton for lining

Pins

15cm (6in) of elastic cord

Two pieces of wool felt or boiled wool, each 10 x 20cm (4 x 8in)

Approx. 2cm (¾in) button (or bigger)

HOW TO MAKE A SASHIKO STITCH AND PATCH SEWING BOOKLET

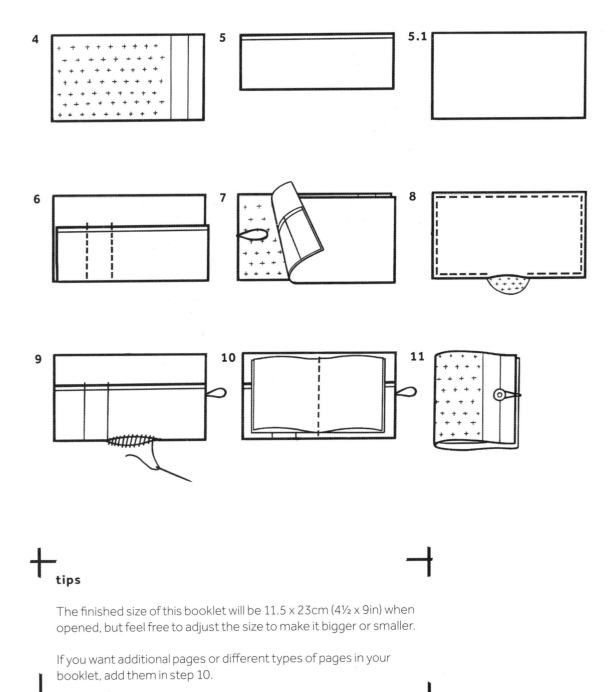

$+$ tips

The finished size of this booklet will be 11.5 x 23cm (4½ x 9in) when opened, but feel free to adjust the size to make it bigger or smaller.

If you want additional pages or different types of pages in your booklet, add them in step 10.

1 Transfer the sashiko patterns on pages 152–154 onto the indigo or dark fabric using a water-soluble fabric pencil (see page 45 for how to transfer the design). If you wish, you can also draw your own design.

2 Once you have the drawn lines on the cloth begin stitching the sashiko pattern in white thread, beginning at one corner of the cloth and taking care to make the stitches and the spacing consistent. Continue working until your sashiko design is complete.

3 Next sew the pieces of remnant fabric together to form a patchwork in any configuration you like (see pages 124–127 for patchwork instructions), such as a series of squares, triangles or strips. Use 1cm (⅜in) seams to create a piece of patchwork measuring approx. 2.5 x 14cm (1 x 5½in). You can hand sew the patchwork using backstitch (see page 18) or use a sewing machine.

4 Once finished, sew one short side of the sashiko fabric to one long side of the patchwork with right sides together and a 1cm (⅜in) seam and then iron all the seams flat. This is the cover for your booklet.

5 Make a 5mm (¼in) hem along one long edge of the interior pocket fabric. With the right side of both pieces facing up, lay the pocket on top of the lining piece so the long raw edge and both raw side edges are aligned. Pin in place.

6 Sew a series of lines down from the hemmed edge of the pocket to the bottom edge to form pocket divisions. Make as many as you like, but I would suggest only one or two on one half of the lining, so that you have a variety of different sized pockets.

7 Place the lining on top of the cover with right sides together. Make sure both pieces are aligned properly all around, with the patchwork portion to the right-hand side and the interior pocket facing up. Pin together if necessary. Fold the elastic cord over into a loop and insert it between the layers in the centre of the opposite end to the patchwork, with the loop facing inward and about 2.5cm (1in) of the ends poking out of the side.

8 Starting on the bottom edge, sew around the perimeter with a 1cm (⅜in) seam allowance, leaving a 5cm (2in) gap in the seam midway along the bottom. As you sew, make sure you secure the ends of the elastic cord.

9 Snip little triangles out of the corners so they lay flat when finished and tie the loose ends of the elastic into a knot so it won't easily pull out. Turn the piece right side out through the unsewn gap at the bottom and press the edges with an iron. Sew the gap closed using slip stitch (see page 19).

10 Measure the width of the booklet cover inside to find the centre point and make a small mark near the top. Place the two felt pages on the inside of the booklet with the centre of the pages aligning with the centre of the cover, making sure to centre them top to bottom as well. Sew through all layers down the centre of the booklet to secure the pages in place.

11 Fold the booklet in half. Pull the loop of the elastic around to the front of the booklet and mark where the button should go. Sew on the button (see page 21).

PROJECT REUSE

loop scarf with flat fell seam

Every studio has piles of fabric remnants waiting for a new project, and since I do a lot of patchwork I tend to save cuttings of all different types and sizes. I use the medium to heavyweight fabrics for patching bags or home accessories, which means I have a lot of lighter weight fabrics still looking for a purpose. This loop scarf is the perfect project because it is entirely composed of smaller bits of lightweight fabric. Inspired by Korean Bojagi textiles, the scarf uses a method of joining small remnants that results in a stained glass effect and the flat fell seams mean that both sides are good. I hand sewed the scarf, which I found quite meditative, but you can easily use a machine if you want to speed things up. I also decided to make it as a loop because I liked how it created a wonderful shape that wrinkles over time, but again, feel free to leave it straight if you prefer.

tools and materials

Pieces of lightweight remnant fabric in a mix of colours, 1.4m (1½yd) in total

Fabric scissors

Sewing needle and thread to coordinate with fabric

Thread snips

Sewing machine (optional)

Seam roller or iron

1 Choose a number of fabrics that make interesting colour combinations in a variety of sizes. Lay out the entire scarf on a table prior to sewing to organize your work. Think of it as made up of blocks, each about 33cm (13in) wide and varying in length, combining to an overall length of about 152cm (60in). Each block can be a single piece of fabric, or a combination of different-sized pieces, organized horizontally or vertically. Try to compose each block independently from the next so that the overall appearance has a playful random feel.

2 Remember while trimming pieces for each block to leave them a little larger, because every seam allowance will be 12mm (½in). You can always trim as you sew the pieces together, or add additional pieces as needed, so that the width of each block is consistent.

3 To sew the flat fell seams, place two pieces of fabric right sides together and sew along one edge with a 1.5cm (⅝in) seam allowance. With your scissors, trim the seam allowance along one side of the seam only so that it is now half the width. While it is possible to sew the seam allowance with one shorter side, I find it faster and easier to trim one side afterward.

4 Now take the wider side and fold it over the shorter side, tucking the raw edge underneath. At this point you can press the seam flat with a seam roller or an iron. To finish, sew the seam flat using slip stitch (see page 19) along the folded edge, if sewing by hand, or simply sew along the folded edge if using a sewing machine.

5 Continue to sew the pieces together, using the same technique for each seam, until you have completed each block. Then join the blocks together. At this point you can keep it as a long scarf or sew the ends together to create a loop scarf.

6 To finish, sew a 5mm (¼in) double hem (see page 21) along the outside edges of the scarf, before pressing the entire piece with an iron.

 tips

There are a lot of options for this project. I had a fair amount of natural dye remnants in linen and cotton in various muted colours that I wanted to use, but really any lightweight material will do. I used a combination of lightweight linen and cotton – a quilting weight would also work well, but avoid anything medium to heavyweight.

The finished size of this scarf is approx. 30 x 152cm (12 x 60in) but feel free to make it narrower or shorter.

Laying out the pieces as described in step 1 will help you visualize which parts within each block to sew together first before moving on to the next.

While the seams for this project allow for both sides to be finished and 'good', there may be one side of a fabric piece that has a quality that you prefer. When sewing the pieces together try to match them so that each side has a consistent look.

PROJECT REUSE

patch cushion

This project is a perfect way to use up all those small fabric remnants. The design is about the layering of fabrics of various colours and sizes to create an interesting pattern, and then using a sashiko stitch over the entire surface to hold all the pieces in place. It is a reference to the Japanese tradition of boro, which is fabric built up with several layers that accumulate over time as areas are repaired due to wear and tear, all held together with stitching. The difference here is that we are using this technique to build a new surface and as a means to compose a patchwork. This is definitely a project that is intuitive because it doesn't have any hard structural rules like a traditional quilting, so it allows a lot of freedom with your composition. There are no mistakes in how you lay out your fabric, and because the edges are kept raw it creates a casual look that will soften further over time. In order to unify the surface I kept all the remnants as either squares or rectangles and arranged them and the stitching in horizontal or vertical lines (no diagonals). But, if you like, this could also be made using a variety of shapes and forms.

tools and materials

Assorted linen and cotton fabrics, medium to lightweight, solid colours or prints

Fabric scissors

Sewing pins

45cm (18in) square of calico (muslin)

Sewing thread and needle

Safety pins (optional)

Sashiko thread or stranded embroidery thread (floss)

Sashiko needle or tapestry needle

Sewing machine with zigzag function (optional)

45 x 60cm (18 x 24in) piece of plain linen

45cm (18in) square cushion pad (pillow form)

1 Trim the pieces into various sizes of square or rectangle (unless you want to use shapes) and cut down any large pieces so that they aren't too big. If some of the fabric pieces have clean-cut edges, take a pin and pull out some of the threads so they all have a soft frayed look. This will give it a more organic, yet consistent, look and feel.

2 Lay the calico flat on your table and start placing the fabric remnants on top, playing with different combinations. Layer your fabrics and move colours and shapes around until you have a nice balance. Play around with overlapping and if you have rectangular shapes try placing them in different directions – but try to maintain your structure within a grid format. Make sure to cover the entire surface of the backing with your fabric remnants.

3 Once you have all your fabric laid out, tack (baste) loosely across the whole surface, just enough to hold everything in place to the backing underneath. I find this is a nice way to hold your fabric pieces down while you do the sashiko stitching, but alternatively you can use sewing pins or safety pins.

4 Now start the sashiko stitching (see page 43) on each piece of fabric. I chose an ecru colour cotton embroidery thread (floss) and used three strands, but sashiko or perle cotton threads would also work nicely. Decide which direction you want the stitching to go – I chose lines of horizontal and vertical stitches, reflecting the fabric shapes, but you could work in one consistent direction across the entire surface. The stitches not only secure the individual pieces in place but also provide overall durability as they join all the pieces to the calico beneath.

5 When you have finished stitching the entire surface of the cushion front, trim any pieces that protrude beyond the edge of the backing.

6 Use a sewing machine to work a zigzag stitch around all four edges of the cushion front, as close to the edge as possible. Alternatively work blanket stitch (se page 20) by hand all around, working close to the edge.

7 Cut the linen into two pieces each 45 x 30cm (18 x 12in). Sew a hem along one long side of each piece and then machine a zigzag stitch along the remaining three edges of each piece. Alternatively work blanket stitch by hand along the remaining three edges, working close to the edge.

8 Place the cushion front down on your work surface right side up. Lay the two pieces of linen right side down on top, so that all the outer edges are aligned and the hemmed edges overlap in the centre for the envelope.

9 Sew around all four sides of the cushion with a 1cm (⅜in) seam allowance, either with the sewing machine or by hand.

10 Turn the cover right side out through the envelope opening and insert the cushion pad.

HOW TO MAKE A PATCH CUSHION

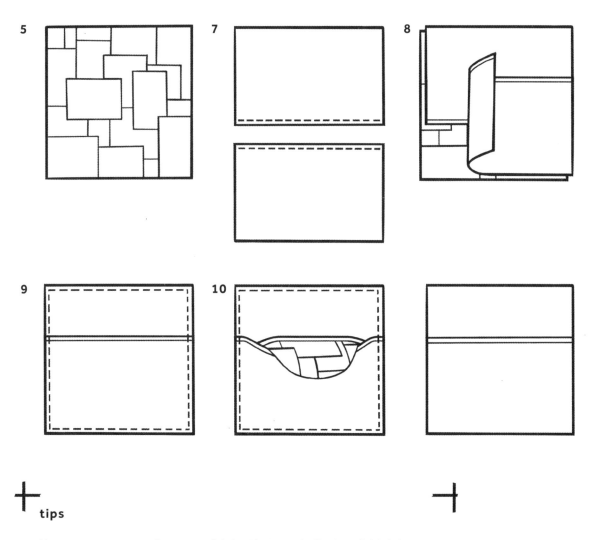

┼ **tips**

Use an assortment of remnant fabrics that are similar in weight. I chose a range of subtle colours but added a few bright ones like yellow as well.

I tend to make my cushion covers a bit smaller than the inserts so that they have a fuller feel.

If you want a bolder look to emphasize the stitching you can use black or even red threads across the entire cushion surface – or you can try different coloured threads in different areas.

PROJECT REUSE

envelope pouch

Everybody needs a little pouch to carry all those everyday small things, and this one is especially useful. It is lined and has one open pocket, with a wrap around cord that acts as a closure. It may be the simplest of designs but it's perfect for your phone or cosmetics, and can also be used as your tool pouch to carry items for your projects. The outside pattern of the design is made up of a grid of small remnants – the ones that usually end up in the waste bin. In my version I used leftover bits of natural dyed fabric arranged somewhat randomly and which I left unadorned. But because this patchwork design is comprised of a series of squares giving it an overall structure, you can give it additional detail by using some of the squares to experiment with colours and patterns. You can even try different appliqué and embroidery techniques.

tools and materials

6.5cm (2½in) square paper template

Remnants of fabric, printed, dyed or both

Fabric scissors

Sewing needle and thread

Sewing machine (optional)

Approx. 20 x 34cm (8 x 13½in) of lightweight fabric lining, such as calico (muslin)

Approx. 20 x 34cm (8 x 13½in) of wadding (batting) (optional)

About 65cm (26in) of leather cord or thin rope

Sewing pins or safety pins (optional)

Sashiko thread

Sashiko needle

HOW TO MAKE AN ENVELOPE POUCH

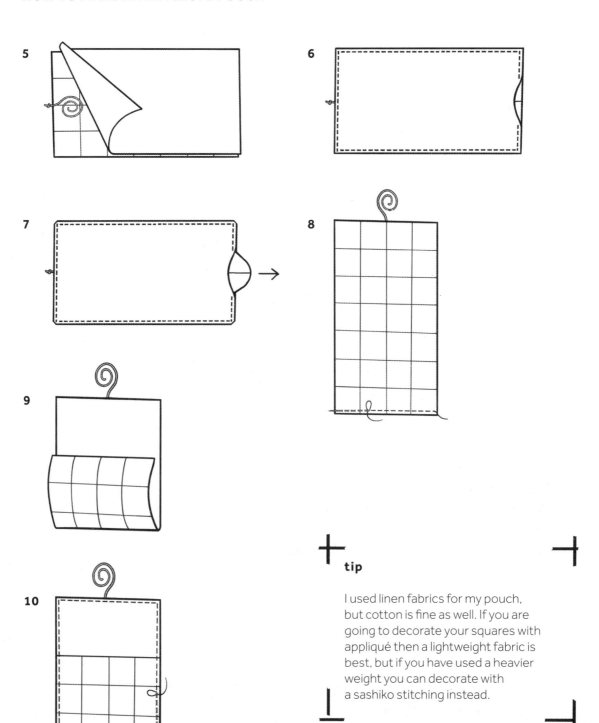

tip

I used linen fabrics for my pouch, but cotton is fine as well. If you are going to decorate your squares with appliqué then a lightweight fabric is best, but if you have used a heavier weight you can decorate with a sashiko stitching instead.

1 Use the paper template to cut 28 assorted squares from the remnants of fabric.

2 Lay out your squares in a rectangle four squares across by seven squares down, in any combination that you find pleasing.

3 Pick up the first two squares across the width, place them right sides together and sew along one edge with a 1cm (⅜in) seam allowance, using a needle and thread or the sewing machine. Open out and press the seam flat. Add the third square to one end in the same way, and then the fourth square. Repeat until you have seven strips of four squares.

4 Now sew the strips together in the same way with a 1cm (⅜in) seam allowance to make a patchwork of four by seven squares. Press all your seams flat.

5 Lay the patchwork down right side up on your table. Knot one end of the cord and place the knot near the edge at the centre of one short side, so it falls within the seam allowance, and the length of cord lies over the patchwork. Place the calico lining on top, and then the wadding (batting) if you are using it. Tack (baste) or pin all the layers securely in place.

6 Leaving a 7.5cm (3in) gap in the seam on the short side opposite the cord, sew the two pieces together all around the edge with a 1cm (⅜in) seam allowance. Make sure the cord is only caught in the stitching at the knot.

7 Snip across the corners and turn the pouch right side out through the unsewn gap along one end. Press the edges with an iron.

8 Using the sashiko thread, work a running stitch through all layers along the short side with the unsewn gap to create a top stitch.

9 Fold the short side that you just top stitched (not the side with the cord) over onto the side with the lining to form a pocket about 11.5cm (4½in) in height. Tack (baste) the corners of the pocket to the back of the pouch so that it doesn't move, or use pins or safety pins.

10 Using the same sashiko thread, work a running stitch through all layers along one side of the pouch to attach the pocket to the back layer, continue up and around to topstitch the flap, then work down the other side.

PROJECT REUSE

bucket project bag

A project bag is one of the most useful little bags you can make. It can be used for your knitting or other crafting supplies, it can be used as a travel bag to organize your packing, or you can use it as a small purse. For this bag I decided to construct the sides by sewing together a series of panels made with fabric remnants – some plain fabric, some printed and some colourful. I've arranged the panels in a casual manner so that the bag has interesting combinations all the way around. But I wanted this design to have a focal point, one spot with a little extra detail, so one panel has a reverse appliqué design with little roundish forms worked like a repeat pattern. As part of the reverse appliqué technique I used small whip stitches all around the forms and further emphasized them with a contrasting thread. The variety of patterns and spots of colour make this a lovely and playful bag and a good way to use up any bits of small fabric you have.

tools and materials

Approx. 24 x 25cm (9½ x 10in) of linen fabric

Pencil

Fabric scissors

Piece of fusible interfacing (optional)

Sewing pins

Black stranded embroidery thread (floss)

Embroidery needle

Mix of linen and cotton remnants, light to medium weight (see tip)

Sewing machine

Approx. 70 x 35cm (28 x 14in) of calico (muslin) or fabric of similar weight

125cm (50in) of leather cord or string

1 Place the template on page 155 onto a window and place the piece of linen on top. Using a pencil trace the shapes onto your cloth. For this appliqué you could now cut out the shapes and leave a raw edge, but if you want to turn under the edges as I have done then draw another line 5mm (¼in) inside the first line as your cutting line. Whichever method you choose, cut out the shapes.

2 If you are turning under the edges, first clip around the inside edge of each opening, making sure not to go over the outside line. Make the clips about 5mm (¼in) apart – this clipping will help the edges stay in shape around the curves.

3 You can either use one piece of cloth to go behind for the reverse appliqué or you can choose different colours from the remnant fabric. I used small bits of grey linen. You can pin the pieces in place behind each opening, or use small scraps of fusible interfacing to hold them in place – making sure to keep them away from the edges so you can still turn these under.

4 Using the tip of your needle to push the fabric edges under, work a whip stitch or small running stitch (see pages 16–19 for stitches) all around the edge of each opening, using three strands of black embroidery thread. Tie off with a finishing knot (see page 56). Continue until the fabric edges are tucked under around each opening.

5 For the coloured panel, cut several small pieces of coloured fabric each 5cm (2in) square and sew them together with a 1cm (⅜in) seam allowance to form a vertical strip 24cm (9½in) high.

6 Sew the coloured strip along one shorter edge of the reverse appliqué panel with a 1cm (⅜in) seam allowance, then add any other strips of printed or plain fabric in the same way to make a front piece for the bag measuring 24cm (9½in) high and 34cm (13½in) long. Refer to the step images on pages 132–133.

7 Join any remnants of printed or plain cloth in the same way with a 1cm (⅜in) seam allowance, to make a back piece for the bag also measuring 24cm (9½in) high and 34cm (13½in) long. Press all the seams flat.

8 Place the front and back pieces of the bag right sides together and sew along the short ends only with a 1cm (⅜in) seam allowance to make a tube.

9 From one of the linen fabrics as used for the reverse appliqué, cut a circular bottom that is 21.5cm (8½in) in diameter for the bag bottom and two pieces of fabric for the drawstring band each 7.5 x 32.5cm (3 x 13in).

10 With right sides together, sew the round linen piece into the bottom opening of the bag. Feel free to pin your pieces together if you need to, for stability when you are sewing. After sewing the bottom piece in, clip into the seam allowance all the way around so the edge will sit nicely when you turn the bag out. Turn the bag right side out.

11 Take the drawstring band pieces and on each short end fold over by 5mm (¼in) twice to make a double hem, then sew close to the first folded edge to hold the hem in place. Fold each piece in half lengthways and sew one to the front and one to the back of the bag with a 1cm (⅜in) seam allowance, making sure they are centred between the main side seams made in step 8. Press the drawstring band pieces flat, so they hang down from the top edge over the right side of the bag.

12 From the calico, cut two pieces 24cm (9½in) high and 34cm (13½in) long for the sides lining, and a piece 21.5cm (8½in) in diameter for the circular bottom lining.

13 Repeat steps 8 and 10 to join the lining pieces, but leave a 7.5cm (3in) gap in one of the side seams so you can turn the bag turn right side out later. Leave the lining wrong side out at this stage.

14 Push the main bag inside the lining, so right sides of both are together and the drawstring band is sandwiched between them. Sew all around the top edge with a 1cm (⅜in) seam allowance.

15 Pull the bag right side out through the gap left in the side seam of the lining. Before pushing the lining down inside the bag, sew up the gap in the side seam with slip stitch (see page 19).

16 Press the bag flat with the drawstring band pointing upward from the top edge. Topstitch (see page 18) around very close to the top edge, just below the drawstring band, to keep the lining in place.

17 Cut the cord into two equal lengths. Thread one round from right to left, so the two ends come out the left side. Knot the ends. Thread the other round from left to right, so the two ends come out on the right side, and knot the ends together.

tip

Your remnants for the patchwork should be in a variety of sizes, some smaller, some larger, with a few pieces of coloured fabrics – I used some natural dye remnants, but you can also use patterned fabric. When combined, they should be equivalent to about 0.5m (½yd) of fabric, but you'll need two pieces at least 7.5 x 32.5cm (3 x 13in) for the drawstring band, and one piece at least 22cm (8¾in) square for the bag bottom.

HOW TO MAKE A BUCKET PROJECT BAG

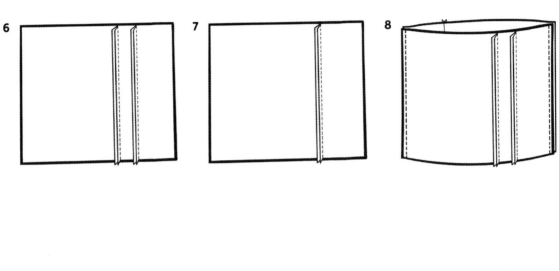

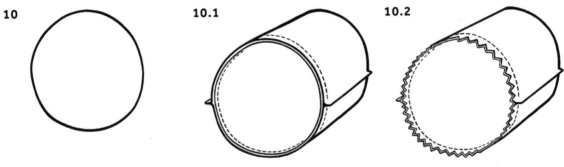

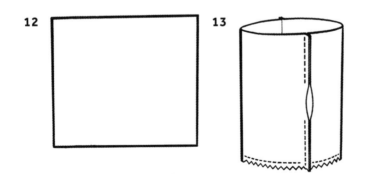

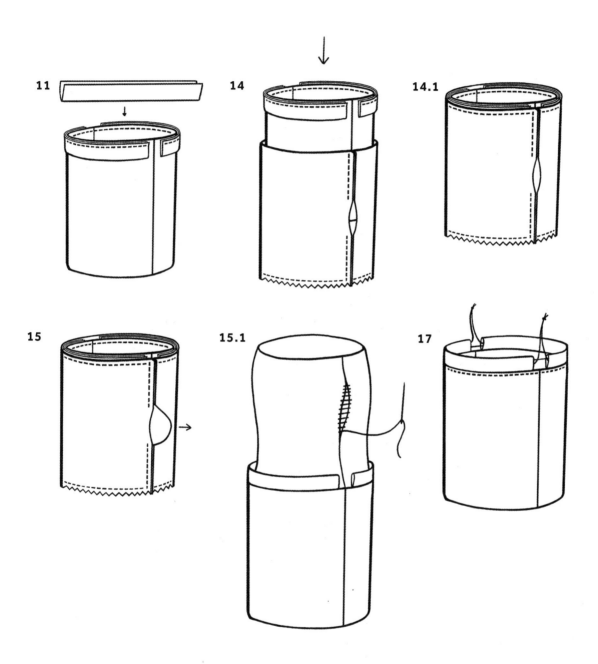

PROJECT REUSE

appliqué cushion

This cushion project uses just a handful of off-cuts from previous projects. It shows that even the smallest amount of fabric, an amount that would normally be discarded, can be used to create simple but lovely designs that make great additions to the places we live. In this repeat pattern I've focused on the repetition of shapes and variations of colour to suggest ways of designing items where modest means can have a big impact. I used a quilting-weight fabric in an array of bright solids to contrast with the dark background and which can be arranged in any number of combinations. Of course appliqué is the obvious technique to use as you can experiment with different combinations, arranging and rearranging, using the actual shapes laid out on the background fabric. Attaching them with a visually subtle stitch lets the formal qualities of the composition really stand out.

tools and materials

Scraps of plain colour cotton fabric, or any lightweight quilting fabric, in a mix of colours

Water-soluble fabric pencil

Fabric scissors

46cm (18in) square of cotton fabric

Pins

Sewing needle and thread

Sewing machine

Overlocker (optional)

2 pieces of linen fabric, each 46 x 30cm (18 x 12in)

46cm (18in) square cushion pad

1 Using the template on page 156 and the water-soluble pencil, trace the double triangle shape onto a variety of coloured fabric scraps. The line that you have traced will be your guide to indicate where to turn under the fabric and helps to maintain a clean and uniform shape for the triangle pieces. Cut the fabric shapes about 5mm (¼in) larger all around than the traced line for the seam allowance.

2 Lay your pieces out and try different combinations to mix and match the colours. When you have paired them up, position the shapes right side up across the right side of the square of fabric for the cushion front – placing them on slightly different angles to create a sense of flow and movement. When you have an arrangement you like, pin or baste the shapes down.

3 To sew the triangular shapes down I used slip stitch (see page19) so that it would not be too noticeable. Fold under the seam allowance of a triangle up to the drawn line and start your slip stitch midway along one side. Bring your needle up through all the layers of fabric, just catching the two layers of the triangle and sew toward one of the corners with stitches every 5mm (¼in) or so.

4 In order to achieve sharp corners, sew right to the point and place a double stitch so that the thread stays in place. Then lift up the layers and snip off a little fabric just on the other side of the point so it's a little less bulky as you fold the next side. Now, right at the point make a little fold straight across perpendicular to the point. Holding the fold down with your finger, fold the second side of the triangle underneath up to the drawn line and continue sewing along the side until you get to the next point.

5 When you have finished stitching all the appliqué, either zigzag stitch around all four edges of the background piece, or sew around with an overlocker if you have one.

6 Sew a double hem (see page 21) along one long edge of both the other two pieces of fabric for the cushion back and then zigzag stitch or overlock the remaining three sides of each.

7 Lay the two pieces right sides down on top of the right side of the cushion front with all outer edges aligned. The hemmed edges of the two pieces for the back will overlap in the centre to form the envelope opening. Sew the back and front together around all four sides with a 1cm (⅜in) seam allowance.

8 Turn the cushion cover right side out through the envelope opening and insert the cushion pad.

HOW TO MAKE AN APPLIQUÉ CUSHION

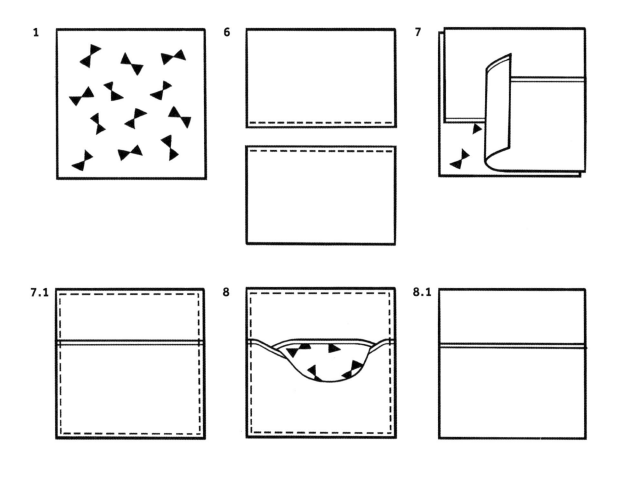

tips

I chose an indigo fabric from a previous project for the background because it was a deep blue that would contrast with the triangle shapes and really let their bright colours glow.

You'll need about 0.25m (¼yd) in total of assorted plain coloured fabrics to make the number of triangles shown in this project.

PROJECT REUSE

indigo-dyed quilt

When making a quilt or a throw you'll need a fair amount of fabric, so reusing old sheets is the obvious choice. And because they are quite often on the light side and faded, they are also the perfect choice for a dyeing project. I chose indigo dye for this piece because I wanted to have a monochromatic colour scheme where I could just have fun playing with lights and darks, and indigo is the one type of dyeing that can easily result in a wide array of tones from a single vat. For this quilt I also wanted to use patchwork – and when I do patchwork I tend to work intuitively, which results in compositions that are less rigid and more organic. So I set up an overall repeating structure that kept everything organized. I dyed four tones of blue, which gave me plenty of material to make any number of patchwork combinations. It works really nicely with the pattern and is a great way to quickly use up those piles of discarded fabric.

tools and materials

2 large buckets, at least 20 litre (5 US gallon) size, one with a lid

Rubber kitchen gloves

Pre-reduced indigo dye kit

Stirring stick

Tarpaulin

Drying rack

Remnant fabric, about two bed sheets each divided into two pieces

Ruler

Fabric scissors

Sewing machine and thread

Iron

Approx. 140 x 155cm (55 x 61in) of cotton wadding (batting)

Safety pins

Sewing needle

Blue quilting thread

1 Following the instructions on your kit, fill one of the buckets with 3–5 litres (approx. 1–2 US gallons) of room temperature water, more if you have a lot of fabric. Wearing gloves to keep your hands clean, mix in the indigo dye followed by the thiorea dioxide and lastly the sodium carbonate (these will be part of the indigo dye kit) – you can mix this first with a little hot water to help it dissolve. Stir the vat gently with a stick to keep air out of the mixture. The vat should be ready in an hour or so after it 'flowers', which is when a foam-like shape has formed in the centre of your vat. You can also leave it overnight before use but remember to keep it sealed with a lid and stored in a warm place.

2 Place your vat on the tarpaulin next to a second bucket filled with clean water, with the drying rack nearby – this should also be on the tarp because there will be a fair bit of dripping. Working with one piece at a time, soak your fabric with clean water and squeeze out the excess. Wearing gloves, dip the fabric into the vat until it is fully submerged and completely saturated – this will only take a few minutes or so – then pull it right out, gently squeezing excess dye back into the vat. It will appear green before turning blue as it reacts with oxygen.

3 After it fully turns blue, rinse it in the water bucket, again squeezing out the excess, before hanging it on the drying rack.

4 Deeper colours are achieved not by a longer duration in the vat, but by dipping the fabric multiple times. So dipping your fabric once as described will give you a light colour, especially after it has been rinsed and dried, while repeating the process will give you a darker colour. As you pull your fabric from the vat between dips, allow the fabric to interact with oxygen for a moment to fully turn blue before dipping once more. There is no need to rinse the fabric in clean water until you are completely finished the dipping process.

5 The quilt is made of strips of patchwork 10cm (4in) wide separated by strips of solid colour 15cm (6in) wide, including a 1cm (⅜in) seam allowance. The patchwork is made only of squares and rectangles, so to give it a more dynamic look I used an overall structure based on the diagonal that starts with a small rectangle in the lower left corner and grows consecutively to the upper right corner. The larger structure creates the pattern, but the patchwork strips allow you to randomly sew pieces of fabric together, small or large, to create playful focal points.

6 Since I dyed four tones of blue, I chose the second to lightest for the main 'background' colour on the 15cm (6in) strips, which left me a light and two darks for the patchwork. Start by cutting a 15 x 25cm (6 x 10in) background blue rectangle for the lower left corner.

7 Now sew pieces of the light and two darks together to create two patchwork strips long enough to be sewn above and to the right side of the lower left corner rectangle. When sewing patchwork I try not to dwell on composition – I use fabric in a wide variety of sizes with a few areas made up of small pieces while others are made up of larger pieces. There are no hard rules in making either the 10cm (4in) wide strips or the 15cm (6in) wide strips – the only dimension you need to think about is the width of the strips and if your fabric piece is not long enough, just sew pieces together to make up the difference.

8 Continue this process, sewing background blue strips followed by patchwork strips. You can use the photograph on page 139 as a guide, but really it's best just to do your own thing when it comes to making up the patchwork strips. Keep going until the overall size of the quilt front is about 137 x 152cm (54 x 60in).

9 When it is finished, lay the front down on a large table and check the overall dimensions, because it may be a little crooked after all that sewing. Trim the edges a bit to square it up if need be.

10 Take the remaining large pieces of dyed fabric and sew them together in any configuration to make the back side of the quilt – but be sure to make it slightly larger all around than the front. You can trim this after you sew the layers together. Press all your seams flat with an iron.

11 Lay the back piece right side down on your table, followed by a layer of cotton wadding (batting) and then the quilt front facing right side up on top. Using safety pins, attach all three layers together to stabilize everything as you quilt the layers together.

12 While there are many ways to quilt visibly, I decided to use a running stitch along the seams of the patchworked areas, using blue thread to minimize its visual appearance. When you have finished stitching, trim the other layers to match the quilt front, if necessary.

13 Lastly, cut 5cm (2in) strips in various tones of blue for the edge binding, and join them together to make one long length of at least 3m (3¼yd). Bind all around the edge of the quilt as explained on page 32–33.

tips

The pre-reduced indigo dye kit can be purchased at most art supplies stores.

Determining depth of colour with indigo dyeing is not an exact science and it takes some experience but, simply put, by multiple dips you can achieve a progression of tones. I achieved the four different tones for this project by making one dip to four dips on my four separate pieces of fabric.

PROJECT REUSE

wearable art

I have always enjoyed trying as many techniques as possible – which is perfect when creating textile art pieces, where many different materials, techniques and ideas can work together in a single project. This is especially true with collage – the art of assemblage – where there is meaning in joining, combining and attaching; where all the parts speak for themselves and contribute to something new. For this project I wanted to make small samplers, no larger than the palm of my hand, where I could combine different techniques to make decorative pieces. I chose patching and embroidery, organized with a recurring half-circle shape. An attached cord is integrated into the pieces to create necklaces. However, any combination of techniques will do and these pieces could easily be made into other accessories, such as patches or pins. Whatever you choose to make, making assemblages out of remnants, scraps of fabric, found objects or collections of stitchwork speaks to the idea of handwork and the meaning of handmade.

tools and materials

Scraps of remnant fabric

Sewing needle and thread

Water-soluble fabric pencil

Fabric scissors

Stranded cotton embroidery thread (floss)

Embroidery needle

Thread snips

Wool roving for stuffing

Small ring or washer

Thin leather necklace cords, or string, ribbon or thin rope

OVAL NECKLACE

1 Choose two pieces of remnant fabric in different colours and hand stitch them together with a 1cm (⅜in) seam allowance. Press the seam open.

2 Lightly trace the oval template on page 156 onto the front of the piece, so that the seam is horizontal and each colour is roughly half of the oval. Cut out the oval shape. This will be the finished size of the piece including a 5mm (¼in) seam allowance.

3 Create some linear details in the lower half of the oval, such as lines of running stitch (see page 16) using embroidery thread (floss) in a contrasting colour. You do not need to carry the stitches all the way to the very edge of the shape, just make sure you finish each line of stitching within the seam allowance.

4 Use the half-circle template to cut a small half circle of fabric – any colour will do, but I chose a subtle variation to the background colour. Place the half circle right side up onto the upper half of the oval with its base aligned with the horizontal seam. Tucking the edges under as you work, sew in place using slip stitch (see page 19).

5 For the back of the piece, cut a single piece of fabric similar in size to the front. Place the front and back right sides together and sew around the edge of the oval with a 5mm (¼in) seam allowance, leaving a 4cm (1½in) gap in the seam somewhere along the edge. Snip into the seam allowance on the curves so they will lie flat when the piece is turned right side out.

6 Pull right side out through the gap and press flat with your fingers. Insert some wool roving through the gap to give the piece a bit of shape. You could also place a few pennies inside to weigh it down so it hangs nicely. Close the opening using whip stitch (see page 19).

7 Sew the ring or washer overlapping the top of the oval, using embroidery thread (floss) and sewing through all the layers to hold it firmly in place. Fold the cord in half and thread the loop through the washer, then bring the two ends up through the loop.

8 Overlap the two ends, and then knot each end over the cord – this creates two sliding knots, so the length of the necklace will be adjustable.

tips

This project is great for all the little pieces of fabric you never know what to do with.

You could add beads, or small found objects such as washers, bits of costume jewellery or found things in nature like twigs, seedpods or stones.

Feel free to adjust the size and the shape of the templates as you wish.

BLUE NECKLACE

1 For the front and back pieces, use the template with the round bottom and cut out the shape twice from a single piece of fabric. This will be the finished size of the piece including a 5mm (¼in) seam allowance. Use the half-circle template to cut a small half circle in a contrasting colour fabric.

2 Position the half-circle shape in the lower half on the right side of the front piece, so it is right side up with the flat edge facing up. Tucking the edges under as you work, sew in place using slip stitch (see page 19).

3 Reflect the half-circle shape by creating an area of stitching above, using embroidery thread (floss) and couching stitches (see page 47). For the horizontal lines use all six strands of a colourful thread – I used yellow – held down by three strands of a contrast thread – I used black.

4 Place the front and back right sides together and sew around the edge with a 5mm (¼in) seam allowance, leaving a 4cm (1½in) gap in the seam somewhere along the edge. Snip into the seam allowance on the curve so it will lie flat when the piece is turned right side out. Finish as in step 6 of the oval necklace.

5 Fold the cord in half and overlap the loop over the centre of the top short straight edge. Using black embroidery thread (floss), sew whip stitch (see page 19) over the loop of cord to attach it to the fabric. Finish the cord ends as described in step 8 of the oval necklace.

RECTANGULAR NECKLACE

1 Choose two pieces of remnant fabric in different colours – I used two closely related shades of grey – and hand stitch them together with a 1cm (⅜in) seam allowance. Press the seam open.

2 Lightly trace the rectangle template on page 156 onto the front of the piece, so that the seam is vertical and each colour is roughly half of the rectangle. Cut out the rectangle shape. This will be the finished size of the piece including a 5mm (¼in) seam allowance.

3 Use the half-circle template to cut two small half circles in contrasting colour fabrics. Position one half circle on the right-hand side of the lower half of the rectangle, with the flat edge along the vertical seam. Position the other half circle above it facing the other way. Tucking the edges under as you work, sew both pieces in place using slip stitch.

4 Reflect the half circles with matching areas of stitching – I used a running stitch in black embroidery thread (floss), altering the direction for each area.

5 Attach the back and stuff as in step 4 of the blue necklace. Find the middle of the cord and attach it all around the edge using whip stitch in black embroidery thread (floss). Finish the cord ends as described in step 8 of the oval necklace.

tip

If you want to make a pin rather than a necklace, omit the hanging cord and sew a large safety pin or kilt pin to the top or back of the piece instead.

templates

**BUTTERFLY APPLIQUÉ
PAGE 66**

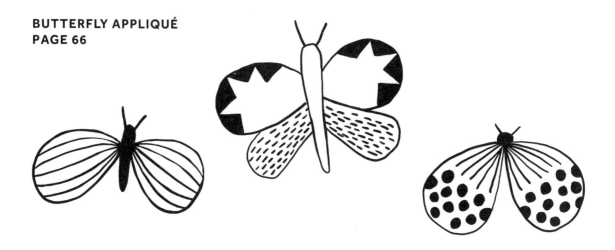

**EMBROIDERED DRESS
PAGE 100**

MAKING FELT PATCHES
PAGE 96

**EMBROIDERY ON MITTS
PAGE 104**

**BLOCK-PRINTED SWEATSHIRT
PAGE 108**

SASHIKO STITCH AND PATCH SEWING BOOKLET
(ALTERNATIVE PATTERN)

SASHIKO STITCH AND PATCH SEWING BOOKLET
PAGE 112

SASHIKO STITCH AND PATCH SEWING BOOKLET
PAGE 112

BUCKET PROJECT BAG
PAGE 128

APPLIQUÉ CUSHION
PAGE 134

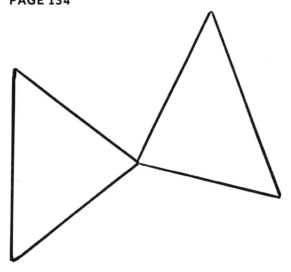

WEARABLE ART
PAGE 144

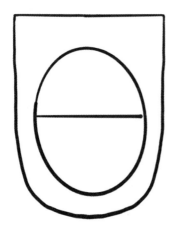  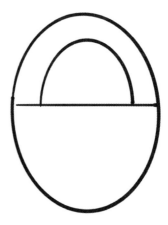

resources

NORTH AMERICA

Tapestry wool, embroidery floss, scissors, magic paper
dmc.com/us

Scissors
studiocartashop.com/products/new-black-silhouette-scissors

Wool embroidery thread
valdani.com/products/

Sulky Stick 'n' Stitch
sulky.com/catalog/sub/sulky-stick-n-stitch

Dealer locator for Clover products: chibi darning needle set, water-soluble pencil, thimbles
clover-usa.com/

Wool darning egg/mushroom
halcyonyarn.com
knitting/70590100/wood-darning-egg
Vintage shops

Natural dye
maiwa.com/pages/natural-dyes

Wool felt
benziedesign.com

Double stick tape and glue
Can be found at any hardware store or craft store

UNITED KINGDOM

Tapestry wool, embroidery thread, scissors, magic paper
www.dmc.com/uk

Tapestry wool, embroidery thread, transfer paper, thimbles
www.woolwarehouse.co.uk

Tapestry wool, embroidery thread
anchorcrafts.com/en

Sashiko threads, fine wool threads, darning mushrooms, needles
tribeyarns.com

Wool darning egg/mushroom, water-soluble pencil
Amazon.co.uk
JohnLewis.com

Natural dye
Wildcolours.co.uk

Wool felt
Woolfeltcompany.co.uk

Double-sided tape and glue
Any craft shop

JAPAN

Natural dye embroidery thread
shop.temaricious.com

Sashiko threads, fine wool threads, needles
daruma-ito.co.jp/products

Tapestry needles
en.tulip-japan.co.jp/handstitch

about the author

Arounna Khounnoraj is a Canadian artist and maker working in Toronto, the city she emigrated to with her family from Laos at the age of four. While her education includes a master's degree in fine arts in sculpture and ceramics, her experiences eventually led to a career in fibre arts – where she focused on a range of printing techniques for textiles, as well as embroidery, patchwork and punch needle. In 2002 she started bookhou with her husband John Booth, a multi-disciplinary studio where she creates utilitarian textile objects such as bags, home goods and textile art.

Arounna has explored a wide range of techniques, methods and materials that express a passion for everyday creativity and the importance of the handmade in everyone's life. Her work emphasizes slow design, intuitive thinking and the importance of handwork. She teaches workshops on a variety of fibre arts and crafts, both in Canada and internationally. She also collaborates with magazines, blogs and artists in creating social media and DIY projects. Her first book, **Punch Needle,** was released in 2018.

acknowledgements

Thank you to everyone at Quadrille Craft especially Harriet Butt, Claire Rochford and Katherine Keeble for helping me create this wonderful book. Thank you also to Marie Clayton for helping me edit the book.

To all the people who support me from near and far, my dear friends, the Booths and all of you who follow my creative journey on social media – your positive energy makes my everyday brighter. Thank you to Kevin, Julie, Ariane, Alex and Gillian for providing me pieces to mend for the book.

To my children Lliam and Piper, thank you for sharing my enthusiasm for making and for modelling my projects in the book.

And a big thank you and lots of love to John for your endless support in life and business and for helping me make sense of my words. I am truly lucky to have you to share in the joy of creating this book and without you by my side none of this would be possible.

Publishing Director Sarah Lavelle
Senior Commissioning Editor Harriet Butt
Head of Design Claire Rochford
Design and Art Direction Katherine Keeble
Photographer Arounna Khounnoraj
Head of Production Stephen Lang
Production Controller Katie Jarvis

Published in 2020 by Quadrille,
an imprint of Hardie Grant Publishing

Quadrille
52–54 Southwark Street
London SE1 1UN
quadrille.com

Cataloguing in Publication Data: a catalogue record for
this book is available from the British Library.

text © Arounna Khounnoraj 2020
photography and artworks © Arounna Khounnoraj 2020
design © Quadrille 2020

Reprinted in 2020, 2021
10 9 8 7 6 5 4 3

ISBN 978 1 78713 610 6

Printed in China